Gyalshen Milü Samleg

Commentary on
Bringing Dreams onto the Path
from
The Compassionate Sun of the Mother Tantra

མ་རྒྱུད་ཐུགས་རྗེ་ཉི་མའི་སྐྱེ་བ་ལམ་དུ་ཁྱེར་བའི་འགྲེལ་པ་བཞུགས་པ་ལེགས་སོ།

Oral Teachings by
Drubdra Khenpo Tsultrim Tenzin

28th December 2021 – 1st January 2022

Transcribed and edited by
Carol Ermakova & Dmitry Ermakov
Illustrations by Yungdrung Rabten

Public Series A

Text Copyright © Tsultrim Tenzin, Carol Ermakova, Dmitry Ermakov 2022.

Illustrations and photos © Foundation for the Preservation of Yungdrung Bön, 2022.

Cover and book layout © Dmitry Ermakov, 2022.

All rights reserved.
This book is in copyright. No part of this publication
may be reproduced, stored in a retrieval system
or transmitted in any form or by any means whatsoever without the
prior permission in writing of the publisher, nor be otherwise
circulated in any form of binding or cover other than that in
which it is published without a similar condition,
including this condition, being imposed on
the subsequent purchaser.

To ensure the ongoing quality and authenticity of Yungdrung Bön practices and teachings, no part of this publication may be translated into any other language without written permission from Drubdra Khenpo Tsultrim Tenzin, Carol Ermakova & Dmitry Ermakov.

Persons attempting to upload this book onto Internet sharing websites such as Scribd will be blacklisted and prevented from acquiring similar materials in the future.

Footnotes, Tibetan terms & Wylie transliteration by Dmitry Ermakov.
Illustrations by Yungdrung Rabten.
Title page photo by Carol Ermakova.
Shenhla Wökar & Gyuma Chenmo thangka photos
courtesy of Christophe Moulin. Sangchog Tharthug Gyalpo thangka includes computer
graphics by Dmitry Ermakov.

This Special Edition has been produced with permission from and in
collaboration with the original publisher FOUNDATION for the
PRESERVATION of YUNGDRUNG BÖN

གཡུང་དྲུང་བོན་ཉར་ཚགས་རིག་མཛོད།
www.yungdrungbon.co.uk

Published 2023 by
Vajra Publications Inc.Pvt.Ltd.
Jyatha, Thamel, P.O. Box 21779, Kathmandu, Nepal
Tel.: 977-1-5320562
e-mail: vajrabooksktm@gmail.com
www.vajrabookshop.com

ISBN 978-9937-624-22-0

Contents

Preface vi
Sixfold Path of the Mother Tantra 1
1. Tsalung and Tummo 4
2. Dream Yoga 6
   Preparations 6
   Main Practice 8
      Body posture 8
      Dreaming and Karmic Causes 9
         Six Chakras and Six Realms 9
            Chakra at the soles of the feet 10
            Chakra at the secret place 10
            Navel Chakra 11
            Heart Chakra 11
            Throat Chakra 12
            Crown Chakra 12
            Bardo 13
   Summary 14
   Dream Yoga in Tantra and Dzogchen 16
   Dream and illusion 17
   Result of Dream Practice 20
      1. Greatness (chewa) 20
      2. Multitude (mangwa) 20
      3. Goodness (zangwa) 21

    4. Swiftness (nyurwa) 21

    5. *Accomplishment (drubpa)* 22

        6. Transformation (gyurwa) 23

        7. Emanation (trülpa) 23

        8. Travelling (dropa) 23

        9. Seeing (thongwa) 24

        10. Meeting (threpa) 24

        11. Experience (nyongwa) 24

The Sixteen Good Qualities of the Path 25

Eleven Examples of Illusion 26

    1. Reflection 27

    2. Water bubble 28

    3. Lightning 29

    4. Rainbow 30

    5. Magic 30

    6. City of scent-eaters 31

    7. Echo 31

    8. Mirage 32

    9. Optical illusion 32

    10. Water Moon – a moon reflected in water 33

    11. Illusion 34

How to Practise Dreams 37

    Meditation on ngöndro 37

        1. General Preliminaries 37

        2. Common Preliminaries 39

        3. Particular Preliminaries – The Short Practice of the Threefold Active Contemplation from Mother Tantra 40

| i. Guru Yoga 42
| ii. *Yidam* Yoga 42
| a) Establishing the Boundary and Dispelling Obstacles 42
| Visualise your mind as a black HUNG / ཧཱུྃ. 42
| b) Requesting Consideration 43
| c) Taking Refuge 45
| d) Generating Bodhicitta 45
| e) Prayer to the Lama and Khandro 45
| f) Mandala Offering 45
| g) Contemplation 46
| h) Yidam Yoga 46
| i) Khandro Yoga 47
| j) Prayer of aspiration 48
| Dream Yoga Preliminaries 50
| i) Body Posture 50
| ii) How to take refuge 50
| iii) How to develop *bodhichitta* 51
| iv) How to pray 51
| 4. Special Preliminaries 51
Aspiration of taking dream as a path 53
The Four Obstacles to Dream Practice 56
Q & A Session 61
Main Practice – how to hold your dream 63
 1st session 64
   The key point of the condition 65
     a) Disturbed sleep 65

b) Obstacle of not being able recognise dreams 66
   2nd session 67
   3rd session 68
   4th session 68
   Training with the Wisdom of Dreams 70
   Developing Dreams 73
   Q & A Session 76
Obstacles to Dream Yoga 77
   1. Sejyam 78
   2. Jejyam 78
   3. Thruljyam 78
   4. Gyujyam 78
The Four Trainings 79
   1. Training with clarity 79
   2. Training with appearances 79
   3. Training with objects of sound 79
   4. Training with objects of vision 79
Sublime contemplation 83
   1. Integration 83
      Integrate all appearances as dream 83
      Maya 84
      Milam bardo 85
   2. Sublime contemplation 86
Four Obstacles to Dream Yoga 89
   1. Thruljyam – Dreams of delusion 89
      Antidote: 89

2. Gyujyam 90
    Antidote: 90
3. Sejyam 91
    Antidote: 91
4. Jejyam 91
    Result 92
Q & A Session 93

Preface

The teaching presented in this book is an edited transcript of a retreat given by Drubdra Khenpo Tsultrim Tenzin, Abbot of the Meditation School at Triten Norbutse Monastery, Kathmandu (28.12.2021 to 01.01.2022). Broadcast via video link from Nepal, the retreat was organised by Shenten Dargye Ling, France and dedicated to instructions from the Mother Tantra of Yungdrung Bön on taking dreams as the path.

    Although this book has been made public following Khenpo's explicit wish, anyone who seriously wants to apply these methods must seek an authentic master and receive the authorisation and transmission in person. This will give the practitioner the ability to clearly understand the meaning of these instructions and connect him/her to the blessing of this lineage, thus ensuring their practice bears fruit.

We hope and pray that this publication will bring benefit to beings!

Thatsen Mutsug Marro! ཐ་ཚན་མུག་ཏུག་མར་རོ༎

Dmitry Ermakov,
North Pennines, UK,
20/04/2022

Welcome to my teachings, everybody.

Today I will be teaching how to practice Dream Yoga according to the Mother Tantra.[1] The text I am using is a commentary by Milü Samleg[2] on the Dream Yoga practice[3] in Magyu.[4]

Sixfold Path of the Mother Tantra

This is quite a big text. Magyu, the Mother Tantra, contains many different teachings, and in particular there are six very important teachings known as *thab lamdrug*,[5] the Sixfold Path of the Mother Tantra. Dream Yoga, or *miwa lamchyer*[6] as we call it, is the second of these six. The six paths are as follows:

1. *Thab lamchyer*[7] or *tsalung* and *tummo*.[8] I was teaching on this last year.

Thab lamchyer is needed for developing and working with prana-mind. This is the first method, *tsalung* and *tummo*. So if you practise *tsalung* and *tummo* very well, finally this practise enables you to

---

[1] For brief history of Mother Tantra see: Tenzin, Drubdra Khenpo Tsultrim. Trnscr. & Ed. Carol Ermakova & Dmitry Ermakov, Illustr. Yungdrung Rabten. *Magyu Tsalung and Tummo: Clear explanations on the daily practice of tsalung and tummo from the Mother Tantra, which is both an excellent medicine for healing hundreds of diseases and the essential elixir of immortality* (UK: FPYB, 2018), pp. 7-13.

[2] Tib. Rgyal gshen Mi lus bsam legs / རྒྱལ་གཤེན་མི་ལུས་བསམ་ལེགས།

[3] Tib. Ma rgyud thugs rje nyi ma'i rmi ba lam du khyer ba'i 'grel pa bzhugs pa legs sHo / མ་རྒྱུད་ཐུགས་རྗེ་ཉི་མའི་རྨི་བ་ལམ་དུ་ཁྱེར་བའི་འགྲེལ་པ་བཞུགས་པ་ལེགས་སྷོ།

[4] Tib. Ma rgyud / མ་རྒྱུད།

[5] Tib. thabs lam drug / ཐབས་ལམ་དྲུག

[6] Tib. rmi ba lam khyer / རྨི་བ་ལམ་ཁྱེར།

[7] Tib thabs lam khyer / ཐབས་ལམ་ཁྱེར།

[8] Tib. rtsa rlung gtum mo / རྩ་རླུང་གཏུམ་མོ། See Ibid.

transform your mind and subtle wind or subtle prana into the *yidam*[9] body, *gyulü*.[10]

2. *Miwa lamchyer*, 'Taking Dreams as the Path to Nirvana.' You usually call this Dream Yoga.

If you practise Dream Yoga very well, finally you can transform your dream body, *milamgyi lü*,[11] into the *yidam* body.

3. *Nyensa lamchyer*,[12] or 'Taking Power Places as the Path to Nirvana'. This encourages you to practise.[13] If you want to practise Tantra and really want to become a Tantric practitioner but your practice is only so-so or you are rather lazy, then you should go to a *nyensa*, a power place and practise where spirits such as *sabdag, lu, nyen* and ghosts[14] gather . If you go there and practise for example *chöd*,[15] 'offering of one's body,' this will stimulate your practice. Why? Because you will feel very frightened in such a place and so there is no way you can be lazy; you will practise very well, day and night. Because you are so afraid, it will be difficult for you to fall asleep so you will practise. Maybe you can see some demons or ghosts and they will frighten you. This is 'the path of encouragement.'

4. *Phenpa lamchyer*.[16] This is the practise of *phowa*[17] for oneself, to transfer one's mind to another body.

Phowa is transference: If your body becomes damaged or doesn't last very long, then you can practise *phowa*, and if you practise very well

---

[9] Tib. yi dam / ཡི་དམ།
[10] Tib. sgyu lus / སྒྱུ་ལུས།
[11] Tib. rmi lam gyi lus / རྨི་ལམ་གྱི་ལུས།
[12] Tib. gnyan sa lam khyer / གཉན་ས་ལམ་ཁྱེར།
[13] Drubdra Khenpo uses 'encouragement' here in the sense of stimulation, something that stimulates one to practise more intensely.
[14] Tib. sa bdag, klu, gnyan, srin po / ས་བདག སྐྱུ གཉན། སྲིན་པོ།
[15] Tib. gcod / གཅོད།
[16] Tib. 'phen pa lam khyer / འཕེན་པ་ལམ་ཁྱེར།
[17] Tib. 'pho ba grong 'jug / འཕོ་བ་གྲོང་འཇུག

and properly, then you can transfer your mind into another body, the body of a recent corpse that is without any damage or disease. If you can find such a body, then there is no need for you to take rebirth in the normal way. Being reborn takes a long time but through *phowa* you can directly transfer your mind into a new body, a body which is already grown up, so it is faster.

5. *Chiwa lamchyer*[18] – *bardo*[19] practice. It is very very important to practise this at the time of one's death.

If you practise *bardo* very well, then finally you are able to transform your *bardo* body, *bardoi lü*,[20] into the *yidam* body.

6. *Nyipa lamchyer*,[21] or sleeping yoga. This is similar to Dream Yoga in that both are practised while one is sleeping, but the goals are different.

In this case, *nyipa lamchyer*, yes, you are asleep, but mainly you are practising with primordial awareness, *rangjyung yeshe*, *rangdrol yeshe*.[22] Or we say *wösal*[23] – Clear Light: *wö* is light and *sal* is clarity, i.e. the Natural State. The main goal here is to practise the Natural State while you are asleep. If you practise this very well, you can easily realise *detong yeshe*.[24]

These teachings are all very, very important.

---

[18] Tib. 'chi ba lam khyer / འཆི་བ་ལམ་ཁྱེར།
[19] Tib. bar do / བར་དོ།
[20] Tib. bar do'i lus / བར་དོའི་ལུས།
[21] Tib. gnyid pa lam khyer / གཉིད་པ་ལམ་ཁྱེར།
[22] Tib. rang 'byung ye she, rang rig ye she / རང་འབྱུང་ཡེ་ཤེས། རང་རིག་ཡེ་ཤེས།
[23] Tib. 'od gsal / འོད་གསལ།
[24] Tib. bde stong ye shes / བདེ་སྟོང་ཡེ་ཤེས།

1. Tsalung and Tummo

This combined practice is extremely important for our meditation. We say it is *srogshing*[25] which means 'pillar.' Why? Because this practice is essential, like the pillar which supports a house. A house cannot stand without the pillar, and we say that *tsalung* and *tummo* are like a pillar because they form the basis for all other practices.[26]

According to Tantra, to reach the Final Goal[27] one must practise two aspects: *chyerim* and *dzogrim*.[28] Maybe everybody knows these. There are also the Three Contemplations:[29]

Contemplation of the Natural State

Contemplation of compassion

Contemplation of the *yidam*.[30]

These three are very, very important for a practitioner of Tantra.

According to Tantra teachings, the two aspects of the Final Goal are realisation of the *yidam* body, *gyulü*, and *detong yeshe*, the wisdom of

---

[25] Tib. sroh shing / སྲོག་ཤིང་། – literally 'tree of vitality'. In cosmology it refers to the World Tree (Tib. dpag bsam ljon shing/ དཔག་བསམ་ལྗོན་ཤིང་།) growing in the centre of the World Mountain (Tib. ri rab / རི་རབ།). In a person it refers to the Central Channel (Tib. rtsa dbu ma / རྩ་དབུ་མ།). In the representations of Buddha's Body, Speech and Mind (Tib. sku gdungs / སྐུ་གདུངས།) it refers to a central pillar or stick wrapped up with mantras which is inserted in the centre of *chörten* (Tib. mchod rten / མཆོད་རྟེན།), which represents Buddha's Mind, or a statue (Tib. sku gzugs / སྐུ་གཟུགས།), which represents Buddha's Body. Buddha's Speech is represented by the texts.
[26] For detailed teachings on *tsalung* and *tummo* see footnote 1.
[27] I.e. Buddhahood, Tib. mngon sangs rgyas pa / མངོན་སངས་རྒྱས་པ།
[28] Tib. bskyed rim, rdzogs rim / བསྐྱེད་རིམ། རྫོགས་རིམ། – generation and completion stages of Tantra.
[29] Tib. ting 'dzin rnam gsum / གཏིང་འཛིན་རྣམ་གསུམ།
[30] Tib. de bzhin nyid kyi ting nge 'dzin, kun tu snang ba'i ting nge 'dzin, rgyu'i ting nge dzin / དེ་བཞིན་ཉིད་ཀྱི་ཏིང་ངེ་འཛིན། ཀུན་ཏུ་སྣང་བའི་ཏིང་ངེ་འཛིན། རྒྱུའི་ཏིང་ངེ་འཛིན།

bliss (*dewa*) and emptiness (*tongpa*).³¹ This is extremely important. Why? Because if you obtain the *yidam* body without *detong yeshe*, then that *yidam* body is just like a dead body. If you realise *detong yeshe* without the *yidam* body, it doesn't work properly as *bardo* consciousness. If at last you are able to obtain *yidam* body, you must bring *detong yeshe* into this body.

All six sections of this Sixfold Path give rise to *detong yeshe*; they are the cause by which one can develop *detong yeshe*.

There are three causes for *yidam* body.

Lungsem,³² or 'prana-mind.' This means that you work with prana and mind and finally your mind changes and becomes *yidam* body. What is prana-mind? We all have mind, and without prana, mind cannot work. You cannot think, you cannot do anything. Subtle mind and subtle prana are the cause of *gyulü*, the illusory body. This is the first thing.

Milamgyi lü, or dream body. This can also be the cause of *yidam* body, because the final goal of Dream Yoga is to change your dream body to the *yidam* body. If you practise very well, daytime and night-time, you can finally change your dream body into the *yidam* body.

Bardoi lü. When somebody dies, there is a period before they take another rebirth, and this is called *bardo*. Beings in *bardo* do not have a body of flesh. They have an empty body, like a dream body, and this *bardo* body can also be the cause for *yidam* body.

There are these three. These are very, very important.

---

³¹ Tib. bde ba, stong pa / བདེ་བ། སྟོང་པ།
³² Tib. rlung sem / རླུང་སེམས།

2. Dream Yoga

Today I am teaching the second path, *miwa lamchyer*. You call this Dream Yoga, and everybody has heard of it. But we call it *miwa lamchyer*, Taking Dream as the Path. Last year I taught the main teachings of *tsalung* and *tummo*. There is also another section, on Sixteen Great Obstacles,[33] which is very necessary but I did not have time to teach it last year. Maybe some other time. Anyway, this year I am teaching *miwa lamchyer*.

Preparations

According to this text, if you very much want to practise Dream Yoga, you need to do a retreat. So first of all you need to go to a quiet solitary place that is not disturbed by humans or dogs.

Once you find such a place, you should refrain from talking. In ancient times there was no internet, no mobile phones, no connection in this way. Now everybody has a mobile phone, internet etc. and this is a big obstacle for practitioners. Here, it says you should cut off and avoid whatever distracts you from your practice, so you should switch off your mobile phone, switch off the internet and just have one or two or three or four good practitioner friends.

First of all, you need to know how to practise Dream Yoga before you go to a solitary place. In other words, you need to receive teachings from a qualified lama, a qualified teacher. And then you need to keep quiet, and stay in silence without talking to each other day or night.

You also need to prepare everything you will need, such as clothes, food, water, firewood and so on. These things are very necessary for a practitioner in a solitary place.

---

[33] Tib. gag sel bcu drug / གག་སེལ་བཅུ་དྲུག

Once everything is ready, you should perform the Magyu *ganapuja*. But it is quite big. Yongdzin Rinpoche is always saying we need to do Magyu *ganapuja*, and in the monastery we do it many times, but it takes two days; it is quite a big ritual.

Then you need to pray to your Root Master.

In the solitary place, you should recite the mantra of the *yidam*:

བསོ་ཨོཾ་པུས་པ་ལི་དྷ་བ་དྷི་ལ་སྭཧཱ།།
SO OM PÜ PA LI DHA WA DHI LA SOHA

Visualise Sangchog Tharthug Gyalpo[34] and offer *ganapuja* to the *dakinis*. There are many Guardians of Magyu, and many of them are *dakinis*.

Then you should develop devotion, *degü*,[35] and the intention to practise. This is very important. You need to have devotion to the lama, *yidam* and *khandro*.[36] If you can, you should do a Magyu *ganapuja*, but if you are alone and you cannot get anything, and can't perform this ritual, then you can do as we always do at the beginning of a session of practice – *Gongchö Namsum*.[37] This also includes the so-called 'body *ganapuja*' or offering one's body. So you can do *mandala* offering to your root lama, offer the body *ganapuja* to Sangchog Tharthug Gyalpo and practise the small *chöd* of the *khandro* as well as practising *chutor*[38] water offering to the four guests[39] once a

---

[34] Tib. Gsang chog Mthar thug rgyal po / གསང་མཆོག་མཐར་ཐུག་རྒྱལ་པོ།

[35] Tib. dad gus / དད་གུས།

[36] Tib. bla ma yi dam mkha 'gro / བླ་མ་ཡི་དམ་མཁའ་འགྲོ། – three objects of Refuge in Tantra.

[37] Tib. Dgongs spyod rnam gsum / དགོངས་སྤྱོད་རྣམ་གསུམ།

[38] Tib. chu gtor / ཆུ་གཏོར།

[39] Tib. mgron po bzhi / མགྲོན་པོ་བཞི། For details on the Four Guests see Ermakov, Dmitry. *Bə and Bön: Ancient Shamanic Traditions of Siberia and Tibet in their Relation to the Teachings of a Central Asian Buddha*, (Kathmandu: Vajra Publications, 2008), pp. 442-448.

8 | Bringing Dreams onto the Path

day. These offerings are extremely important; maybe I will tell you more about them tomorrow.

So, you should practise this way in a place of solitude, and if everything is OK, then you can start practising Dream Yoga.

Main Practice

Body posture

In a comfortable bed, lie down on your right side. Or take any position that is comfortable for you. However, the best position is the sleeping lion posture:⁴⁰

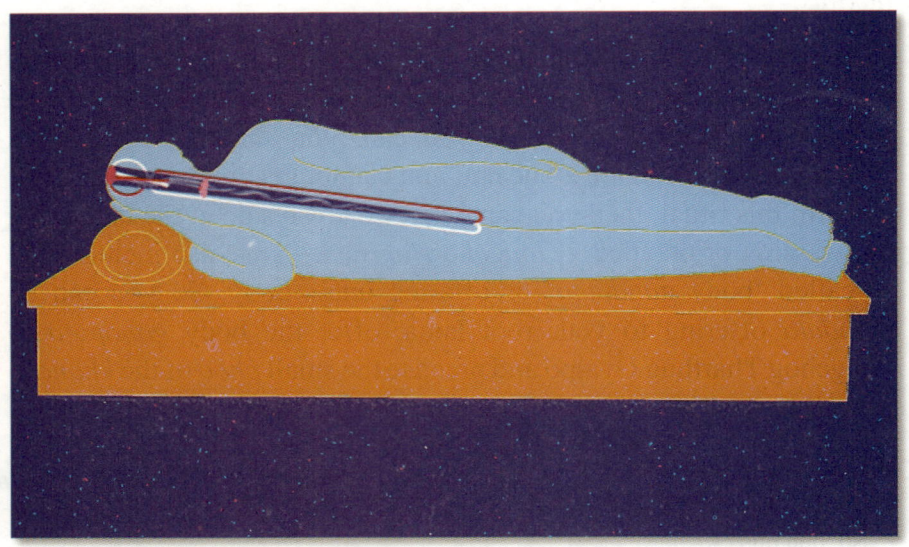

Sleeping lion posture with channels

Lie on your right side.

Cup your right cheek in your right palm.

Rest your left hand on your left hip or thigh.

---

⁴⁰ Tib. seng ge'i nyal stabs / སེང་གེའི་ཉལ་སྟབས།

Put your legs together and bend your knees slightly.

Then go to sleep.

If this position is not comfortable, you can assume any position that is.

Then dreams will come.

Dreaming and Karmic Causes

From beginningless time up until now, each of us has had countless bodies, countless lives, and so we have accumulated many, many various karmic causes. There are three types of karma or *le*[41] in Tibetan:

Connected with virtue, *gewa*[42]

Connected with non-virtue, *migewa*[43]

Connected with neutrality.[44]

Therefore, we talk about good karma, bad karma and neutral karma.

Six Chakras and Six Realms

In our body we have six chakras: crown chakra, throat chakra, heart chakra, navel chakra, secret place chakra and the chakras on the soles of our feet. While we are sleeping, our prana-mind, *lungsem*, can enter these chakras. Within each chakra is the seed syllable for one of the Six Realms.

---

[41] Tib. las / ལས།

[42] Tib. dge ba / དགེ་བ།

[43] Tib. mi dge ba / མི་དགེ་བ།

[44] Tib. lung ma bstan pa / ལུང་མ་བསྟན་པ།

10 | Bringing Dreams onto the Path

So there are six chakras, six seed syllables and six realms.[45] Now we have this body, a human body, and the seed syllables are there. They look like syllables but in fact they represent karma. We are humans but we have the karma of beings in all six realms. That means that we already have the karma for taking rebirth in all six realms, and where we take rebirth depends on our condition; the seed is already there.

Chakra at the soles of the feet

If our prana-mind enters the chakra at the soles of our feet while we are asleep, we have dreams of anger. Anger is the cause of rebirth in the hell realms.

In this case, we can dream of huge fires, massive expanses of water or floods, mighty winds. We may dream that the earth is covered in fire and that our body is terribly hot, as though we were burning in a blazing fire. Or sometimes we might feel terribly cold, like cold wind or icy cold water. Or snow, like on the top of Mount Everest where it is so cold that the snow is permanently frozen. This is the feeling of beings in the cold hells.

If your prana-mind enters the chakra on the soles of your feet, you have dreams of anger. What are these? You dream of killing, of great suffering. You sometimes feel very hot or very cold, or both at once. For instance the top part of your body feels as though it is burning up with a fever while the lower half is terribly cold.

If you have such dreams, it means your prana-mind has entered the chakra at the soles of your feet.

Chakra at the secret place

If your prana-mind enters the secret place, dreams of desire appear to you. We have the Five Poisonous Emotions[46] and these are the cause for rebirth in the different realms. Anger is the cause for rebirth in a hell realm, desire is the cause for rebirth in the hungry ghost realm.

---

[45] See table p. 15.
[46] Tib. dug lnga / དུག་ལྔ། – anger, desire, ignorance, jealousy and pride.

The seed syllable for the hungry ghost realm is in the chakra of the secret place, so if the prana-mind enters this place while you are asleep, you will have dreams of desire. Sometimes you will feel very thirsty, or very hungry. You will crave food or water but not be able to get any. Sometimes you will dream of having sex. If these dreams come, that means that your prana-mind has entered the secret place while you are sleeping.

Navel Chakra

The navel chakra is the chakra of samsara.[47] If your prana-mind enters the navel chakra while you are asleep, you have dreams of ignorance. Ignorance is the main cause of rebirth as an animal. Or an insect, or a water being like a fish or a crocodile. These are all 'animals,' *duddro*.[48] The cause is ignorance, and so now you have dreams of ignorance. You dream of impure things, ocean beings, or of different animals. Maybe that you are riding a horse, or you are with cows, goats or sheep and so on. You might dream of fish, snakes, crocodiles etc. Or of leprosy. In ancient times, in Tibet, this was an incurable disease. But I don't know how it is to dream of leprosy. People used to be very afraid of this disease, so perhaps they dreamt they had this disease themselves. Anyway, these dreams are all signs that your prana-mind has entered the navel chakra.

Heart Chakra

Sometimes the prana-mind enters the heart chakra with the syllable NRI while we are sleeping. It looks like a syllable NRI but actually it represents the seed syllable of human beings. Buddha said that human beings generally have a lot of jealousy, that jealousy is the cause of rebirth as a human, and so we say you have jealous dreams, or dreams of jealousy. This means that you dream of many possessions – houses, cups, human things. Or sometimes you may dream of narrow places. Narrow-mindedness is similar to jealousy, so you may dream of a

---

[47] Tib. 'khor ba / འཁོར་བ།
[48] Tib. dud 'gro / དུད་འགྲོ།

narrow gorge that you cannot pass through, or of falling from a high precipice or a very high rock or mountainside. Or you may dream of slandering others. Sometimes you might dream that you are put in prison by the police or other people, that you are in jail and locked up. If you have this kind of dream, it is a sign that your prana-mind has entered your heart chakra with the NRI syllable. These kinds of dreams are similar to what you do during the day.

Throat Chakra

The throat chakra is the place of the *asuras*. So you see, your body is not just you! The six realms and the six syllables are already there!

If your prana-mind enters the throat chakra, you will have dreams of pride. Pride is the cause of the *asura* beings. So you can dream of many people all gathered together, as in a marketplace, with many people coming and going. Or you may dream of weapons, of guns or spears and lances, long knives, swords – things that soldiers in the army use. You may dream of rival armies fighting, of war. Or of armour and helmets made of iron, and of people fighting. You may also dream of thunderbolts, hail and lightening. If you dream these things, that is a sign that your prana-mind has entered the throat chakra.

Crown Chakra

If your prana-mind enters your crown chakra, the place of the gods – as I said earlier, generally we have five poisonous emotions, and each one is cause for rebirth in one of the six realms. So anger is the cause for hell, desire is the cause for hungry ghosts and so on. If all these passions or poisons are present in equal measure and not so strongly, without one being predominant, and if you have collected many virtues in past lives, then this is the cause for rebirth in the god realm. If your prana-mind enters your crown chakra while you are sleeping, you will dream of singing, dancing, *lugar*.[49] Or you may dream of looking in a mirror and seeing yourself wearing many garlands of

---

[49] Tib. glu gar / གླུ་གར།

flowers. You can dream of flowers, singing, dancing, or of being in a beautiful garden or using good things. If you have dreams like this, it is a sign that your prana-mind has entered the crown chakra, and this is similar to the condition of the gods.

You already have the karma for each of the six realms, and dreams can show you which will predominate in your next life. For example, if you usually have dreams of desire, then that shows you your next life will be in the hungry ghost realm. Or if you have dreams of anger and sometimes feel terribly hot or cold, or see floods or fire or feel hot and cold simultaneously, that means you have more karma of a hell being. If on the other hand you always dream nice dreams, like walking in a garden, seeing many different flowers, or of playing, singing and dancing, then you have more karmic seeds of the gods or *devas*.

Bardo

Generally we say that the *bardo* lasts forty-nine days. However, this is not fixed. Some people may remain in the *bardo* for many years. Sometimes a being is unable to take rebirth and stays in the *bardo* for a very long time, for *kalpa*.[50] In this case, they become a bit like a hungry ghost. But generally, most people stay in *bardo* for forty-nine days and then take rebirth. But who knows what kind of rebirth it will be!

For the first three and a half days after death, a being generally falls into a state that seems like unconsciousness. Then they enter the *bardo*, and remain there for 49 days.

The first week is the *bardo* of hell. The experience is similar to when we dream of hell. This *bardo* situation feels very similar, but actually we are in *bardo*.

---

[50] Tib. bskal pa / བསྐལ་པ། – aeon.

The second week is the *bardo* of hungry ghosts. The experience is similar to when we dream of the hungry ghost realm. This *bardo* situation feels very similar, but actually we are in *bardo*.

The third week is the *bardo* of animals. The experience is similar to when we dream of the animal realm. This *bardo* situation feels very similar, but actually we are in *bardo*.

The fourth week is the *bardo* of humans. The experience is similar to when we dream of the human realm. This *bardo* situation feels very similar, but actually we are in *bardo*.

The fifth week is the *bardo* of *asuras*. The experience is similar to when we dream of the *asura* realm. This bardo situation feels very similar, but actually we are in *bardo*.

The sixth week is the *bardo* of gods. The experience is similar to when we dream of the god realm. This *bardo* situation feels very similar, but actually we are in *bardo*.

The seventh week is real *bardo*.

It is like that. So during the *bardo*, our experiences can feel like when we are dreaming. You can check these feelings yourself.

Summary

So to sum up, in a retreat of Dream Practice, you:

Offer a Magyu *ganapuja*

Pray to your Root Lama

Perform *Gongchö Namsum* offering

Check your dreams to see which are predominant, and this is similar to *bardo*.

CHAKRA	SYLLABLE	REALM	EMOTION
Crown	A	Gods/Hla	All emotions in equal proportions
Throat	SU	Demigods/Hlamin	Arrogance/Pride
Heart	NI	Human beings	Jealousy/Envy
Navel	SU	Animals	Ignorance/Sloth
Secret place	TRI	Hungry ghosts	Attachment/Avarice
Soles of feet	DU / DU / DU	Hell beings	Anger

Dream Yoga in Tantra and Dzogchen

This is very, very important. Whether are you a Dzogchen practitioner or a Tantra practitioner, whatever you do, Dream Practice is very important. Why? Because in Magyu it is written: 'wherever there is smoke, there is surely fire.' So that means that you need to recognise your dreams while you are asleep so that you can practise the Natural State, or your *yidam*, or compassion etc. while you are dreaming, sleeping. If you can remember your practice while you are dreaming, then you can remember your practice in the *bardo*. It is a good sign. And if you can remember or recognise your practice in the *bardo*, that is of very great benefit.

If you practise very well in this life but can't remember anything in the *bardo*, then at that moment whatever rebirth you take is determined by karma. If on the other hand you remember your practice when you are in the *bardo*, you can control your rebirth yourself, you are free and can choose where to be reborn.

So now, in this life, if you don't recognise you are dreaming or don't remember your practice or meditation while you are sleeping, then you won't remember in the *bardo*, either. If on the other hand you do remember now, while you are dreaming, then for sure you will be able to remember in the *bardo*. That is another reason to practise Dream Yoga.

I have already mentioned the main goal of Dream Yoga according to Tantra. In Dzogchen, the main goal is to recognise awareness of Dzogchen in the *bardo*, not to obtain *yidam* body and *detong yeshe*. The nature of mind mentioned in Tantric teachings is similar to the Natural State of Dzogchen, but it is mixed with thought.

Dream and illusion

Dream is dream! It looks real, but it isn't. For example, if you dream of eating honey, you can taste it is very sweet, but it is just an illusion. You see something that seems real, but in fact it is just like a water in a mirage.

Day and night, you should consider that whatever you see, whatever you think or hear, feel taste or smell is all just *gyuma*, illusion, or dream. There are many, many different universes, but they are all just illusions. You should develop the habit of viewing everything you see or hear etc. as illusion or dream, a mirage.

Everybody has experienced dreams. But in fact, even though whatever you see or think or feel during the daytime seems real, the teachings of Dzogchen and Tantra say everything is just empty form.[51] What does 'empty form' mean? First, things appear from emptiness, now they abide in emptiness and if they disappear, there is nowhere else, they disappear into emptiness.

Think this again and again.

In dream practice, during the daytime, consider whatever you see, hear, smell, taste etc. as dream. This is very, very important.

For example, if during the daytime you think again and again that everything is dream, empty form, then this is the method whereby you can recognise your night-time dream as dream. But if you don't think during the day very strongly that everything is dream, illusion, mirage, if you don't really think this strongly, then you won't be able to recognise you are dreaming at night.

This is a very, very important point. Daytime visions are all as dreams. Meditate on this: everything is as dream.

Practise in this way – this type of thinking is also practice, very good practice! For example, if you are very happy today, consider it is a

---

[51] Tib. stong gzugs / སྟོང་གཟུགས།

dream. Or if sometimes you are suffering, your mind is very upset or you don't feel so good, that is great suffering, *dugngal*.[52] But if you consider your sufferings as merely an illusion, a mirage, a dream, then that will help you feel better.

Really, it is like an illusion, nothing lasts for long. Just some time. Maybe you are suffering, it will pass. Maybe you are not suffering now, you feel happy, but that can change a lot. Everything is illusion. Human beings' condition is illusion.

Whatever actions you do, whatever activities you perform, even compassion and devotion – these are all illusion. Bodhichitta and compassion are also illusion but *rigpai rangzhin*,[53] nature of awareness, cannot be illusion. So if you have some nice things, some nice times and you are happy, consider that this is all illusion, too.

If you do this every day, reminding yourself that whatever you see, whatever you hear, whatever you own is all illusion, a dream, then if you are a good Tantric practitioner, some *dakini* may come to you in your dream and guide you to paradise, just as they appeared to masters of the Shen lineage.[54] There was a very great yogi of the Shen lineage, Shen Nyima Gyaltsen,[55] and the *dakinis* were always leading him to paradise in his dreams, while he was asleep, Or sometimes we can have daydreams, visions, and if you practise very well, *yidams* or *dakini* can come to you in your visions. We call this *nyamnang*,[56] or experiential visions. Pure or impure, both. If you are a good Tantric practitioner and you practise *chyerim* and *dzogrim* very well, then maybe *yidams* and *dakini* will visit you in a dream.

---

[52] Tib. sdug bsngal / སྡུག་བསྔལ།

[53] Tib. rig pa'i rang bzhin / རིག་པའི་རང་བཞིན།

[54] Tib. Gshen tshang / གཤེན་ཚང་།

[55] Tib. Gshen Nyi ma rgyal mtshan / གཤེན་ཉི་མ་རྒྱལ་མཚན། – b. 1360. He established Triten Norbutse Monastery (Tib. Khri brtan Nor bu rtse / ཁྲི་བརྟན་ནོར་བུ་རྩེ།) in Tsang (Tib. Gtsang / གཙང་།) province of Central Tibet.

[56] Tib. nyams snang / ཉམས་སྣང་།

But whatever your dreams, if you consider everything as illusion, that is of great benefit. Why? Because desire will diminish, gradually becoming less and less. If you have a vision or dream of a *yidam*, that might make you very happy, and then that happiness leads you to samsara. Suffering! So you should consider everything, even this, as illusion, as dream.

Practise this way, day and night. Remember this again and again, whatever you do, whether you are eating, drinking, walking, in a bus, in the car, in the cinema – in the cinema you can see a very good example of illusion. In Tibetan we say *lognyen*,[57] 'reflection of electricity.' It is very very important to think about this because if you want to be aware in your dreams, and recognise that you are dreaming, first you need to practise in this way, again and again, and finally you will be able to recognise your dream, and ultimately attain Buddhahood. This is the final goal for a practitioner of Tantra. Also for practitioners of *tsalung* and *tummo*, the final goal is to obtain *gyulü* and *detong yeshe*.

What do I mean by 'recognise your dream?'

For example, when I sleep, I dream. Maybe I dream I'm going somewhere, and now in the dream I recognise: 'Oh, I am dreaming! Wherever I go now, I am dreaming.' This is 'recognising your dream.' Most people can't do this. Or sometimes you just start to recognise your dream, and then you wake up, and sleep is gone.

---

[57] Tib. glog brnyan / སློག་བརྙན།

Result of Dream Practice

There are eleven results:

Greatness, multitude, goodness, swiftness, accomplishment, transformation, emanation, travelling, seeing, meeting, experiencing.

1. Greatness (chewa)[58]

Your body is small compared to a mountain, but if you recognise you are dreaming, you can change your body into a large body, make it as big as a mountain. You can imagine your body is very, very big. At the moment you have small knowledge, small realisation, but one result of Dream Yoga is that you can change this into great knowledge.[59] You can transform yourself to be as big as a mountain, with great knowledge.

2. Multitude (mangwa)[60]

You have one body but you can emanate many bodies. Or if you only know one subject, you can multiply this so you know many things. In this way, you can have 100, 1000 bodies with inconceivable knowledge.

Or if you dream that you have one cow, you can change that cow into many cows, and then you can change all those cows into Buddhas! Many Buddhas, not just one. If you can recognise your dream, while you are dreaming you can transform your cow into Buddha, the cow becomes Buddha, you can see it as Buddha. This can be useful in the *bardo*, too.

If you dream of a woman, you can transform her into a *dakini*. If you dream of a boy, you can transform him into a *pawo*,[61] an awareness-holder. It is very difficult to recognise the *bardo* state, but if you train in this way, maybe in the *bardo* you will see a cow, then you recognise

---

[58] Tib. che ba / ཆེ་བ།
[59] Tib. chen po'i yon tan / ཆེན་པོའི་ཡོན་ཏན།
[60] Tib. mang ba / མང་བ།
[61] Tib. dpa' bo / དཔའ་བོ།

this as a *bardo* vision, then you can transform the cow into your *yidam* and it will immediately change and become Sangchog Tharthug Gyalpo. You will see it as your *yidam*. So the dream state and the *bardo* state are very similar.

3. Goodness (zangwa)[62]

Ordinary sentient beings are not good; they are often quite the opposite, bad. This is because they are deluded, always. But if you practise Dream Yoga, you can change these ordinary sentient beings into beings with good qualities. In your dream, you can make good qualities appear from these ordinary beings. Generally, all sentient beings have many bad qualities, such as negative emotions, delusions, ignorance, confusion, obscurations, defilements, thoughts etc., but in the dream, you can change these into good qualities. You can even change sentient beings into Buddha.

4. Swiftness (nyurwa)[63]

Generally, we only dream for a short time, but in that short time, you can have so many different dreams. For example, before I wake up I have a very clear dream. Then I wake up. But during this dream – it is only a very short time, maybe five or ten minutes – I have a lot of dreams and it feels like the activity of 24 hours. If you recognise this, then in that short time you can progress along the path very fast. I told you already, in Magyu we have the Sixfold Path, and this is the Second Path. Generally we talk about the Five Paths,[64] the Ten Bhumis,[65] the

---

[62] Tib. bzang ba / བཟང་བ།

[63] Tib. myur ba / མྱུར་བ།

[64] Tib. lam lnga / ལམ་ལྔ།: tshogs lam, sbyor lam, mthong lam, sgom lam, mi slob pa'i lam / ཚོགས་ལམ། སྦྱོར་ལམ། མཐོང་ལམ། སྒོམ་ལམ། མི་སློབ་པའི་ལམ། – 1. Path of Accumulation, 2. Path of Unity, 3. Path of Vision, 4. Path of Meditation and 5. Path of No More Learning i.e. Buddhahood. For details see: Yongdzin Lopön Tenzin Namdak Rinpoche, Trnscr. & Ed. Carol & Dmitry Ermakovi. *The Nine Ways of Bön: A Compilation of Teachings in France, Volume I, Bön of Fruit*, (France: Shenten Dargye Ling, 2006), pp. 126-129, 137-142.

[65] Tib. sa bcu / ས་བཅུ།: rab tu dga' ba'i sa, dri med shel gyi sa, 'od zer 'phro ba'i sa, phyag rgya bsgyur ba'i sa, bon nyid sprin tshogs sa, bde ldan rtogs pa'i sa, yid bzhin

Ten Paramitas[66] and so on, and in the dream, you can progress very quickly because you can practise these things in a very short time. It is not possible to do this during the day.

5. *Accomplishment (drubpa)*[67]

There are things that you cannot do during the daytime, the waking state, but if you recognise your dream, you can do them in the dream state. For instance, I can't drive a car or a motorbike. But in a dream, I can. So it is like this. Here, many people can't climb to the top of Mt. Everest, but in a dream, everyone can! This is achievement or accomplishment. Attainment. Another example: in the daytime, we can't speak to animals, but maybe we can in a dream. Maybe you can communicate with animals, gods, hell beings, hungry ghost and so on. You can't do this during the daytime, but if you recognise your dream, you can communicate with them, and you can also do whatever the gods or *devas* can do.

'grub pa'i sa, ma chags dag pa'i sa, yi ge 'khor lo'i sa, mi 'gyur g.yung drung sa / རབ་ཏུ་དགའ་བའི་ས། དྲི་མེད་ཤེལ་གྱི་ས། འོད་ཟེར་འཕྲོ་བའི་ས། ཕྱག་རྒྱ་བསྒྱུར་བའི་ས། དོན་ཉིད་སྤྲིན་ཆོགས་ས། བདེ་སྤྱན་རྟོགས་པའི་ས། ཡིད་བཞིན་འགྲུབ་པའི་ས། མ་ཆགས་དག་པའི་ས། ཡི་གེ་འཁོར་ལོའི་ས། མི་འགྱུར་གཡུང་དྲུང་ས། – 1. Bhumi of Excellent Joy, 2. Bhumi of Immaculate Crystal, 3. Bhumi of Radiant Light Rays, 4. Bhumi of Transforming Mudra, 5. Bhumi of the Billowing Clouds of the Nature of Existence, 6. Bhumi of the Realisation of Bliss, 7. Bhumi of the Fulfilment of all Wishes, 8. Bhumi of pure Non-Attachment, 9. Bhumi of the Wheel of Letters, 10. Bhumi of the Immutable Swastika. For details see Ibid. As well as Tr. Nagru Geshe Gelek Jinpa, Carol Ermakova & Dmitry Ermakov. དུ་ཏྲི་སུའི་སྒྲིབ་སྦྱོང་གི་སྒྲུབ་གཞུང་མུན་སེལ་སྒྲོན་མ་འཁོར་བ་དོང་སྤྲུགས་བཞུགས།། THE LAMP WHICH DISPELS DARKNESS: the practice manual of DU TRI SU which purifies defilements and dredges all beings from the depths of Samsara, TIBETAN-ENGLISH, SECOND EDITION, (FPYB & Shenten Dargye Ling, 2018), pp. 213-230.

[66] Tib. pha rol tu phyin pa bcu / ཕ་རོལ་ཏུ་ཕྱིན་པ་བཅུ་: sbyin pa, tshul khrims, bzod pa, brtson 'grus, bsam gtan, stobs, snying rje, smon lam, thabs, she rab / སྦྱིན་པ། ཚུལ་ཁྲིམས། བཟོད་པ། བརྩོན་འགྲུས། བསམ་གཏན། སྟོབས། སྙིང་རྗེ། སྨོན་ལམ། ཐབས། ཤེས་རབ། – 1. generosity, 2. moral discipline, 3. patience, 4. diligence, 5. meditative concentration, 6. power/strength, 7. compassion, 8. wish-fulfilling-prayer, 9. method, 10. wisdom. For details see: Ibid. Ibid.

[67] Tib. grub pa / གྲུབ་པ།

6. Transformation (gyurwa)[68]

If you dream of a lion, for instance, you can transform your body into the lion. Or a dragon. In Tibet we have three favourite animals: snow lion, dragon and *garuda*.[69] The snow lion is always on snowy mountains, the *garuda* is always in space, but I am not sure about the dragon. Tibetans think that if there is rain and thunder in the summertime then that is the dragon roaring. So you can transform into one of these three, or you can change your body to that of the *yidam*, to Sangchog Tharthug Gyalpo. Or if you dream of a woman, you can transform her into a *dakini* and let her guide you to paradise. You can visit paradise, go there as a tourist!

7. Emanation (trülpa)[70]

Now your body is your normal body, but if you recognise your dream, you can emanate as a noble body – as a god or *deva*, or a Buddha body, for instance. This is like *yilü*,[71] a mental body, one kind of illusory body.

8. Travelling (dropa)[72]

In your dream you can go to paradise, or to a special place, Gaden,[73] a happy place of the gods where everything is very beautiful. Or you can go to Olmo Lungring.[74] Maybe you have all heard of Olmo Lungring. According to Yungdrung Bön[75] history, Tönpa Shenrab[76] was born there. So you can go there in a dream and visit Tönpa

---

[68] Tib. 'gyur ba / འགྱུར་བ།
[69] Tib. khyung / ཁྱུང་།
[70] Tib. sprul pa / སྤྲུལ་པ།
[71] Tib. yid lus / ཡིད་ལུས།
[72] Tib. bgrod pa / བགྲོད་པ།
[73] Tib. Dga' ldan / དགའ་ལྡན།
[74] Tib. 'Ol mo lung ring / འོལ་མོ་ལུང་རིང་། – birthplace of Tönpa Shenrab, Buddha of Yungdrung Bön.
[75] Tib. G.yung drung bon / གཡུང་དྲུང་བོན།
[76] Tib. Ston pa Gshen rab mi bo / སྟོན་པ་གཤེན་རབ་མི་བོ།

Shenrab. Or you can go to the *yidam*'s place and visit your *yidam*. In the mandala of Magyu there are 366 deities, and you can go and visit them. This is the result of travelling.

9. Seeing (thongwa)[77]

In a dream, you can see something you have never seen before. For example, you can see all the Buddhas of the Ten Directions. All the *sugatas*,[78] the Buddha places, Indra's place and so on. Bönpo texts say that many, many gods live on the top of Mount Meru, including the Hindu gods Indra, Shiva and Vishnu. Hindus say their gods reside on Mount Kailash. So in your dream, you can see whatever you want to see, gods and so on. There were many *siddhas*[79] and teachers in ancient times, and in a dream you can visit Tapihritsa or Nangzher Lödpo[80] and so on.

10. Meeting (threpa)[81]

If someone has passed away, you can visit them. Or if you want to meet someone in the future, there is no need to wait, you can see them in a dream.

11. Experience (nyongwa)[82]

In your dream, you can experience things you previously had never experienced. You can experience many things.

These are the Eleven Results of practising Dream Yoga.

---

[77] Tib. mthong wa / མཐོང་བ།

[78] Tib. bder gshegs / བདེར་གཤེགས།

[79] Tib. grub thob / གྲུབ་ཐོབ།

[80] Tib. Ta pi hri tsa, Snang bzher Lod po / ཏ་པི་ཧྲི་ཙ། སྣང་བཞེར་ལོད་པོ། – 25th and 26th masters of Zhang Zhung Nyengyu (Tib. Zhang snyan rgyud / ཞང་ཞུང་སྙན་རྒྱུད།) Dzogchen lineage.

[81] Tib. 'phrad pa / འཕྲད་པ།

[82] Tib. myong ba / མྱོང་བ།

The Sixteen Good Qualities of the Path[83]

Next come the sixteen good qualities of the path.[84] This means that, at that moment, in just a short time, while you are dreaming, you can plish the Five Paths: 1. Path of Accumulation; 2. Path of Unification; 3. Path of Seeing – if you attain this Path, then that is the First Bhumi.[85] If you attain the First Bhumi, then in a short time you can visit 100 Buddhas, you can go to 100 paradises and receive many different teachings.

Thus, if you practise Dream Yoga properly, you can attain these 16 different qualities.

If you have many thoughts in the dream, it doesn't matter; you can take this as the path to nirvana.

If you have many delusions in the dream, it doesn't matter; you can take everything that happens as the path. For example, if you are very afraid, you can change that feeling to happiness. Or if you are deluded or confused, you can change that to wisdom.

The text says we can have many thoughts, many illusions. Dream is also illusion.

This is the benefit of Dream Practice: it is like the wisdom of the First Bhumi. If you attain the first Bhumi, you are an *arya*, you are beyond

---

[83] Tib. lam gyi yon tan bcu drug / ལམ་གྱི་ཡོན་ཏན་བཅུ་དྲུག

[84] This text does not list these qualities but, as Drubdra Khenpo explained below, they are e.g. going to see a hundred Buddhas at the same time, receiving a hundred teachings at the same time, visiting a hundred paradises at the same time etc.

[85] Tib. sa dang po / ས་དང་པོ Five Paths are divided into two categories: 1. Worldly Paths (Tib. Tib. 'jig rten gyi lam / འཇིག་རྟེན་གྱི་ལམ) which include paths 1 & 2; and Beyond Worldly Paths (Tib. 'jig rten las 'das pa'i lam / འཇིག་རྟེན་ལས་འདས་པའི་ལམ) which include paths 3-5. So the third path, the Path of Seeing, corresponds to the First Bhumi, the Bhumi of Excellent Joy. The 4th path, the Path of Meditation, has many subdivisions which correspond to *bhumis* 2-10. The 5th path, the Path of No More Learning is Buddhahood. For more details see: Yongdzin Lopön Tenzin Namdak Rinpoche, Trnscr. & Ed. Carol & Dmitry Ermakovi. *The Nine Ways of Bön, Volume I, Bön of Fruit*, pp. 137-142.

samsara. Samsara is behind you. You are in nirvana. First nirvana. So, the benefit of recognising your dream is like the benefit of attaining the First Bhumi. This is very good. Because you can collect all the good qualities of Buddha. You can change your body into many different forms – *yidams*, *dakinis*, *pawo* etc. You can transform yourself into Drenpa Namkha[86] or Tapihritsa.

This is all according to the Commentary by Milü Samleg.

Eleven Examples of Illusion

Today I want to explain, the Eleven Illusions[87] that serve as examples for the dream state, even though dream itself is illusion.

1. Reflection
2. Water bubble
3. Lightning
4. Rainbow
5. Magic
6. City of scent-eaters
7. Echo
8. Mirage
9. Optical illusion
10. Moon reflected in water
11. Illusion[88]

You can see so many different things in a dream, but whatever you see while you are asleep, all appearances are just dream visions. In the daytime (i.e. the waking state) you can see, hear, taste etc. many

---

[86] Tib. Dran pa nam mkha' / དྲན་པ་ནམ་མཁའ། There were three main emanations of Drenpa Namkha. For more information see: Ermakov, D. *Bø and Bön*, pp. 144-149; https://yungdrungbon.co.uk/2021/03/06/three-drenpa-namkhas-in-yungdrung-bon/
[87] Tib. mthun pa'i dpe sgyu ma bcu gcig / མཐུན་པའི་དཔེ་སྒྱུ་མ་བཅུ་གཅིག
[88] Tib. gzugs brnyan, chu lbur, glog, gzha' tshon, mig 'phrul, dri za'i grong khyer, brag cha, smrig rgyu, mig yor, chu zla, sgyu ma / གཟུགས་བརྙན། ཆུ་ལྦུར། གློག གཞའ་ཚོན། མིག་འཕྲུལ། དྲི་ཟའི་གྲོང་ཁྱེར། བྲག་ཆ། སྨྲིག་རྒྱུ། མིག་ཡོར། ཆུ་ཟླ། སྒྱུ་མ།

things, and while you are asleep you can also see many different things. Many different dream visions appear, and although they look real, they are merely relative truth. What does that mean? It means that you can see them, you can hear them, but they are not real, they have no inherent existence – that is absolute truth.

You see many things during the daytime, too, and these are also merely relative truth. All appearances are relative. It is the same in a dream; things can appear, but they are not real. So we talk about two truths,[89] relative and absolute.[90]

If you practise with Dream Yoga, dream visions can appear as wisdom. Wisdom means the realisation of the Natural State. If you keep in the Natural State, then whatever dream visions appear, they all appear as wisdom awareness. But if on the other hand you cannot recognise dream visions as dream, then they can delude you. So during the daytime you see many things, during the night-time you see many dreams, and this is very similar. Neither exist inherently, yet still they appear and seem real to you. That is why we talk about two truths, relative and absolute. The true Nature of Mind is no different; relative truth and absolute truth are non-dual, inseparable, like water and wet or fire and hot. It is impossible to separate wetness from water or heat from fire. If something is water, it is wet. If something is fire, it is hot. So in the same way, in reality, relative truth and absolute truth are inseparable, even though they may appear different.

1. Reflection

Whatever dream visions you have are all like reflections. You can see so many different reflections in a mirror. Or in water. If you look into water, you can see your face. It looks real but it isn't. So in the same way, many things can appear in your dream, but they lack inherent existence. Therefore we say dream visions are like reflection.

---

[89] Tib. dben pa gnyis / བདེན་པ་གཉིས།
[90] Tib. kun rdzob bden pa, don dam bden pa / ཀུན་རྫོབ་བདེན་པ། དོན་དམ་བདེན་པ།

2. Water bubble

Dream is part of your mind. At night, when you are sleeping, you have a dream, but it is not real. It is just part of your mind. Your mind appears as a dream. So actually, your dream is your mind. Whatever appears in your dream comes from your mind, nothing comes from outside. It is the Nature of your mind, even though the visions may be very diverse. That is why we use the example of a water bubble. Bubbles can be big or small, different shapes, even different colours and so on, but they are all wet. Water. It is like this. Water appears as bubbles, and in the same way, the Nature of your mind appears as dreams. In reality, dream is Nature, and Nature is *semchyi rangzhin*[91] – Nature of Mind.

Many different things can appear. During the day you can see forms with your eyes, hear things with your ears, touch many things etc. and whatever you have experienced, in reality it is all the Nature of your mind. The reality of all these things is the Nature of your mind. The whole universe is also an appearance of the Natural State.

We talk about the Three Great Visions – sounds, rays and lights.[92] First, sounds, rays and lights appear. These lights are like rainbows. The sounds are like echoes. The rays are like the many rays of the sun. So, sounds, rays and lights appear, but the source is the Natural State.

From there, the five elements arise,[93] and the six existences[94] manifest which are perceived by six senses:[95]

---

[91] Tib. sems kyi rang bzhin / སེམས་ཀྱི་རང་བཞིན།

[92] Tib. sgra 'od gzer gsum / སྒྲ་འོད་གཟེར་གསུམ།

[93] Tib. 'byung ba lnga / འབྱུང་བ་ལྔ།

[94] Tib. rigs drug / རིགས་དྲུག

[95] Tib. dbang po drug / དབང་པོ་དྲུག – Tib. mig gi dbang po, rna ba'i dbang po, sna'i dbang po, lce'i dbang po, lus kyi dbang po, yid kyi dbang po / མིག་གི་དབང་པོ། རྣ་བའི་དབང་པོ། སྣའི་དབང་པོ། ལྕེའི་དབང་པོ། ལུས་ཀྱི་དབང་པོ། ཡིད་ཀྱི་དབང་པོ།

- Form – eye
- Sound – ear
- Smell – nose
- Taste – tongue
- Touch – skin
- Mental events – mind

These are the objects of the five senses. There are some forms of existence that we can see but not hear, or hear but not taste, and there are some that we can only understand through our mind, mental consciousness. So mental consciousness is the sixth.

Then the universe appears. This is like a vessel, and all the sentient beings are inside.[96] So all the multiple universes with multitudes of sentient beings appear from sounds, rays and lights. And the sounds, rays and lights appear from the Natural State.

All of these appear from Nature. Dream is similar; whatever appears in a dream seems real, but in fact it isn't real, it has no inherent existence. That is why we talk about relative truth and absolute truth.

Here the text gives the example of an army made up of many different soldiers grouped together.

3. Lightning

Many different things can appear in quick succession in a dream. They possess the energy of self-awareness. The Natural State – *nelug*[97] – has three qualities: clarity, emptiness, and inseparability.[98] We call the

---

[96] Tib. phyi snod, nang bcud / ཕྱི་སྣོད། སྣང་བཅུད།
[97] Tib. gnas lugs / གནས་ལུགས།
[98] Tib. gsal stong dbyer med / གསལ་སྟོང་དབྱེར་མེད།

clarity aspect 'awareness.' Sometimes we say 'empty awareness,'[99] because clarity and emptiness are not separate. We talk about different qualities, but they have the same nature. It is like the examples I gave before of water and wetness, fire and heat. This potential energy of awareness appears very quickly from the Natural State. It is beyond thoughts. We cannot grasp or imagine what kinds of dream visions can appear – many, many different things arise very, very fast, and we say this is like lightning. When lightning flashes in the sky, it never lasts long. Now we are talking about dreams, but actually it is the same in the daytime, too; a lot of things can appear, but they are not real, they don't last long, and so they are like lightning, too.

4. Rainbow

As I have said, a lot of different dream visions arise but nothing is real, nothing exists inherently. If you want to grab hold of something, you can't. You can't touch or hold anything in a dream. That is why we say it is like a rainbow. You can see a rainbow, it looks very nice with various layers of colours, but you can't catch hold of it. If you walk towards a rainbow, it seems to go further and further away, then it suddenly disappears. Dream visions are similar, they appear rapidly but you can't do anything with them. Therefore they are like a rainbow.

5. Magic

In a dream, you can go beyond your bedroom, you can go very far, very fast, and even jump over nine mountains in Zhang Zhung, Tagzig, or you can go around Mount Kailash.[100] Regions of East and South Tibet are a long way from Mount Kailash and in ancient times people though that it was a really long journey, that it would take you a year to get there if you went on foot. There were no vehicles, no cars or planes. And even if you took a horse, the horse would soon grow tired and so people walked, carrying their bags. And it was a very, very long way. But here it says: in your dream you can go to Mt.

---

[99] Tib. stong nyid ye shes / སྟོང་ཉིད་ཡེ་ཤེས།
[100] Tib. Ti se / ཏི་སེ།

Kailash very quickly. Much faster than by plane! Therefore it seems like magic.

6. City of scent-eaters

You can own a great variety of things in a dream – many clothes, houses. We say it is like a story, a fable, like a city of scent-eaters. Scent-eaters or *driza*[101] are beings who are always hungry, but they can only eat scents, smells. Their city looks very nice. There is an area in India that is extremely flat, no mountains or hills, just flat land. It seems as though the sun rises from the earth and sets back into it at night. Sometimes it rains very heavily there, and then stops abruptly. When that happens, you can see a beautiful city. It isn't real but you can see it, very briefly, just for a second or two. Then it disappears without a trace. This is called *drizi drongchyer*,[102] city of scent-eaters. Dreams are similar. Sometimes you might dream of a beautiful city, vast and immeasurable. It looks real, but it disappears without a trace.

7. Echo

If you stand in front of a cliff face or a very high rock and shout something, the rock will repeat what you say. If you practise Dream Yoga properly, you will be able to dream of whatever you want to see. For example, if you want to see paradise or visit some *yidams* or *dakinis*, just before you fall asleep, think very intently about what you want to see, and then go to sleep. If you do this, then whatever you want to see or hear will appear as a dream vision. You can practise like that. I have experience. If for example I want to get up at 6 o'clock one day, I go to sleep and then naturally wake up at 6 am. No need for alarm clock. This is similar. Just before you fall asleep, think very strongly about what you want to see or do in your dream. Don't just think about it once or twice. You have to practise this many times, then maybe you can dream of it. This is like an echo; you say 'hello!' and the rock says 'hello!' You say 'hey!' and the rock says 'hey!' This

---

[101] Tib. dri za / དྲི་ཟ།
[102] Tib. dri za'i grong khyer / དྲི་ཟའི་གྲོང་ཁྱེར།

is similar. Just as the rock says whatever you say, in the same way, the dream answers whatever you want to see. Therefore it is like an echo.

8. Mirage

If you want to go out of your house during the day, you have to go through the door. You can't go out another way. But in a dream, you can go through the wall, you don't need to use a door or window. You can walk through walls, rocks, tables – nothing material can stand in your way. You can walk in the sky, too. Therefore we say it is like a mirage. Mirages appear in very dry, sandy places like Arabia when it rains and the sun is shining at the same time. It looks as though there is some water somewhere, but in fact it is not real. Many wild animals are confused by mirages. They are thirsty, it looks like water, they go towards it, but the water keeps getting further and further away. Then suddenly it disappears. That is a mirage. And this is similar; you can see a lot of different things in your dream, but you can't get to them, you can't touch them.

9. Optical illusion

Sometimes people see things in space that are not really there. They believe they really see something, but nothing is there, nothing is real. In dreams, no matter what you see, nothing is real. That is, *mig'yor* – optical illusion

When you are dreaming, whatever you see is empty form. For example, if you are asleep and you eat honey in a dream, it seems as though you are really eating it, you can taste sweetness, but when you wake up, there is nothing in your mouth, and no sweet taste. It is like this. When you are dreaming, your senses seem to be blocked or turned inwards. For instance, your eyes are closed, your tongue is not tasting anything and yet still everything in you dream seems real. In this way, whatever you see in dream differs from what you see during the day, in the waking state.

10. Water Moon – a moon reflected in water

Whatever you dream, be it good, bad or neutral, nice or nasty, nothing is separate from your mind. It is all just projections of your mind. We say it is like a moon reflected in water; it looks like the moon, but it is only a reflection, so in fact, it is just water. The moon in the water looks as though it is something different or separate from the water, but in fact it is water. In the same way, nothing is separate from your mind. Dream visions are not beyond your mind. If you have no mind, then you have no dreams. We have Eight Consciousnesses,[103] and while we are asleep, everything we see, hear, taste etc. is a mental appearance, a mental vision because it is connected with our mental consciousness and not separate from our mind. Just as a moon reflected in water is not separate from the water.

If you are a good dream yogi, you can change whatever you dream. For example, if you have one dream, you can change it and have many dreams. Or if you dream of fire you can increase that and make a vast fire that covers the whole earth. You can transform everything in this way. If you dream you have a dog, you can turn it into a lion. Or you can transform a small bird into a *garuda*. Or if you want to have a good horse, when something appears in your dream you can transform it into a very good horse and go riding.

In the *bardo*, it is similar. If you practise Dream Yoga very well – this is the teaching of Buddha – then one day when you land in the *bardo* (and for sure we will all go there) it will be like a dream vision. This is very, very similar. So if you have trained well then when you see someone, you can remember to transform them, and then you can see whoever you want to. For example, if you see a man in the *bardo*, you can transform him into Sangchog Tharthug Gyalpo. Or if you see a woman, you can transform her into *dakini* Chyema Wötsö. The *bardo*

---

[103] Tib. rnam shes tshogs brgyad / རྣམ་ཤེས་ཚོགས་བརྒྱད། – the Six Consciousnesses dealt with above plus Tib. nyon yid / ཉོན་ཡིད།, emotional consciousness, and Tib. kun gzhi rnam shes / ཀུན་གཞི་རྣམ་ཤེས།, universal storing consciousness or all-ground consciousness.

is similar to the dream state; you can see many things, and if you just remember, you can change everything by yourself.

11. Illusion

In big towns there are sometimes people who can do this. We call it *gyuma* – a trick or illusion. They take some small stick or pebble, say some spells or something, and change it. Now I will tell you a story. This story is from *Yangtse Longchen*:[104]

> *"Once upon time, long ago, there lived a king who was always thinking about horses. He loved horses, and was always busy with them, so much so that he neglected his people. This King had a great kingdom with many good things, including a very astute minister. This minister thought to himself: 'Our King is always busy with horses, he doesn't take care of his people, so I must try to find a magician for him.' And so the minister made enquiries and asked around, and finally someone told him: 'Yes, there is a man called Gyuma Dega,[105] he can perform tricks, he's a good illusionist.' So the minister asked Dega to do a trick on the King, since he was too preoccupied with horses to care for the people. Gyuma Dega agreed.*
>
> *And so one morning, the servants brought the King his breakfast and laid it out nicely, but just as the King was about to drink his tea, he looked out of the window and saw a merchant with a lot of fine horses approaching the palace. The King immediately wanted to buy one of these nice horses, and so he didn't eat his breakfast but hurried out to the merchant instead. It was Gyuma Dega, who arrived in the guise of a horse merchant, and the King rushed over and began discussing the horses, saying how much he wanted to buy one. When the King asked the price of the best horse, Gyuma Dega said: 'You decide how much you want to pay. First check the horse, go for a ride,*

---

[104] Tib. Yang rtse klong chen / ཡང་རྩེ་ཀློང་ཆེན། – one of the four major Bönpo Dzogchen cycles.
[105] Tib. Sgyu ma bde dga' / སྒྱུ་མ་བདེ་དགའ།

put the horse through its paces, and then decide how much it is worth.'

So the King chose a horse and set off. The horse began galloping. It galloped like the wind and immediately arrived in some strange place that the King had never seen before. The place was deserted, no people to be seen. The King felt very hungry and thirsty but there was nobody around, just the horse. So he kept roaming around on the horse, and he was very frightened, he thought he might fall off!

The whole day passed, and evening came. Just as the sun was about to set, the King saw some smoke. 'Ah, there must be someone there! Look, smoke!' So he went in that direction and saw an old woman with her daughter, and a few sheep and goats. Nothing else. 'Can I stay here tonight?' asked the King. The old woman and her daughter agreed. They gave him some food, and he slept there that night. When he woke up in the morning, he wanted to leave, but he had no idea where he was because he didn't recognise anything, so he stayed there. One day passed. Then another. Then a week. Then another. Months and years passed. The King married the old woman's daughter. They had children. The children grew up. The one day the old woman, his wife's mother, died. His wife was very upset. 'Oh, my only mother has died!' she said. 'Now I want to die, too!' And having said this, she immediately jumped into the nearby lake and drowned. So the old woman and her daughter were both dead. Then the children began calling 'Mummy! Mummy!' and they, too, ran into the water and died.

Now the King was all alone. He cried and cried.

And suddenly his servants asked him 'Why are you crying? What's the matter?' The King told them all about his life, his family, and his great suffering, but the servants were so surprised. 'What are you talking about?' they asked him. 'Look!

> *Here is your breakfast! Your tea is still hot! Only a few moments have passed!'"*

So, this is a story about Gyuma Dega, the illusionist who made tricks, *gyuma*. It is like this. You can see many things in dreams, and if you are a great practitioner, a great dream yogi, you can train and transform whatever appears.

So, this was the teaching on the Eleven Illusions that serve as examples for dream state.

As I have already told you, this teaching is from the Sixfold Path, and there are six *dakinis* who are associated with these Six Paths. Now I am teaching Dream Yoga, the Second Path, and last year I taught the First Path, *Tsalung* and *Tummo*. The *dakini* who owns this path of Dream Yoga is called Gyuma Chenmo,[106] or Great Maya, Great Illusion.

She can control dreams. You can pray to her to help you recognise you are dreaming. This teaching of Eleven Illusions, Eleven Mayas. is from this *dakini*. Her teaching says:

> *"If you practise Dream Yoga properly, finally you can recognise your dream. If you purify your dream by recognising it as such, you can change normal dreams to pure dreams. If you practise Dream Yoga properly, finally you can transform your dreams.*[107] *If you want to multiply things, you can make them increase by themselves. If you meditate on dream, finally you can realise this."*

This is the explanation of what a dream is.

---

[106] Tib. Sgyu ma chen mo / སྒྱུ་མ་ཆེན་མོ།

[107] For example, if you suffer greatly in your dreams, if you can remember and recognise you are merely dreaming then you can change this by yourself into happiness. It is like that.

How to Practise Dreams

Now comes the detailed explanation on how to practise Dream Yoga. There are many subdivisions. I taught these things already.

Wonderful!

Meditation on ngöndro[108]

There are four subdivisions:

1. General Preliminaries
2. Common Preliminaries
3. Particular Preliminaries
4. Special Preliminaries

1. General Preliminaries

This deals with what I mentioned yesterday about finding a suitable solitary place for a Dream Yoga retreat. This place should be isolated, without any people or distractions, without many friends, without your mobile phone or the internet and so on. Just a few people, who agree to practise seriously with you, or just you, in retreat.

a) As for food, you should avoid impure food such as the meat of an animal half eaten by a wolf or dog. We say meat like that is unclean, you may get sick and your mind may become muddled.

b) As for devotion to your lama, you should prepare a good, clean offering. Sometimes people make huge offerings but they are defiled in some way and that spoils the offering. If you are in retreat practising Dream Yoga, you should avoid this.

c) As for the retreat place, you should choose a nice place that is far from people or animals. It should be isolated but pleasant,

---

[108] Tib. sngon 'gro / སྔོན་འགྲོ།

with flowers, trees and grass around it, so your body and mind are comfortable.

d) As for companions, you should avoid friends who distract you.

e) As for *samaya*,[109] generally people have many different *samayas* or vows with their teacher, and if something is broken, you should repair it through confession. There are root and branch *samayas*, and if part of a branch vow is broken, your practice of Dream Yoga will never be successful because the *dakini* Gyuma Chenmo will punish you. She doesn't like you if part of your *samaya* is broken. Breaking a vow is a big mistake, so first you must practise confession to purify or repair any broken *samaya*.

f) Remember the suffering of samsara. Try to develop disgust towards samsara. Usually most people like samsara, they have a lot of desire and want many things, they are attached to samsara. This is their state of mind. But you need to change your mind. As you practise more and more, your mind will gradually change so you become less and less attached to samsara. That is the benefit of your practice. If on the other hand you practise a lot but your mind doesn't change, then that is a sign that your practice is not working very well. So, you should be saddened and sickened by samsara, and remember the benefit of practising.

g) You should practise *yidam* Sangchog Tharthug Gyalpo, both *chyerim* and *dzogrim*. Recite his mantra:

བསྒོ་ཨོཾ་པུས་པ་ལི་དྷ་བ་ཛི་ལ་སྭཧཱ།།
SO OM PÜ PA LI DHA WA DHI LA SOHA

while maintaining the visualisation. This is part of *chyerim* and is extremely important. If you don't practise the *yidam*, if you don't pray to the *dakini*, or if you lack devotion to the Three

---

[109] Tib. dam thsig / དམ་ཚིག

Jewels,[110] then serious obstacles can arise for your practice. For instance, you may start your retreat and then immediately have to go somewhere; that is an outer obstacle. Or you may have many thoughts and feelings while you are in retreat. These are inner obstacles and they are very dangerous because if you can't control your thoughts then they can lead to anger, desire, jealousy etc. and so the Five Poisons arise. That is why it is very important to pray to lama, *yidam* and *khandro* to remove, banish and purify all obstacles.

2. Common Preliminaries

Your retreat place may be far from humans, but the real landlords or owners are spirits – *sabdag, lu, nyen, tod*.[111] We can't see them, but they are there, and if you don't appease them, they can cause obstacles. How can we purify these obstacles?

We do:

Water Offering,[112]

Ganapuja,[113]

Guru yoga,[114]

Yidam yoga.

Simple *chöd* practice etc..

---

[110] Tib. dkon mchog gsum / དཀོན་མཆོག་གསུམ། Drubdra Khenpo explains: usually the Three Jewels refers to Buddha, Dharma and Sangha, but here it refers to Lama, Yidam and Khandro.
[111] Tib. gtod / གཏོད།
[112] Tib. chu gtor / ཆུ་གཏོར།
[113] Tib. tshogs mchod / ཚོགས་མཆོད།
[114] Tib. bla ma'i rnal 'byor / བླ་མའི་རྣལ་འབྱོར།

3. Particular Preliminaries – The Short Practice of the Threefold Active Contemplation from Mother Tantra[115]

Yongdzin Rinpoche often asks us to perform the ganapuja of Magyu, again and again. It is very long practice and takes two days. Or sometimes he asks us to do the fire puja of Chyema Wötsö, and that takes three whole days. However, if it is not possible for you to do these long pujas, then you can perform the short version, *Gongchyo Namsum*, which I will explain now.[116]

There are three sections:

    i. Guru Yoga
    ii. *Yidam* Yoga
    iii. Small *chöd* practice or *Khandro* Yoga.

If you concentrate and visualise everything very well while you are doing these, that will be of great benefit. Otherwise, even if you recite a lot with your mouth, if you don't focus properly, that is not good. What you do with your mind is most important here. Practising devotion to the Three Jewels is very important as your practice won't develop properly without this.

---

[115] Tib. Ma rgyud dgongs spyod rnam gsum bsdus pa bzhugs / མ་རྒྱུད་དགོངས་སྤྱོད་རྣམ་གསུམ་བསྡུས་པ་བཞུགས།

[116] For Tibetan see footnote 115 above. The recitation and text can be found in forthcoming Tibetan-English bilingual edition: མ་རྒྱུད་རྩ་རླུང་དང་གཏུམ་མོ་ཐིག་ལེ་གག་སེལ་བཅས་ཀྱི་ཉམས་ལེན། སྦྱར་བྱ་མཁན་པོ་ཚུལ་ཁྲིམས་བསྟན་འཛིན་ནས་མཛད།, Tenzin, Drubdra Khenpo Tsultrim. Tr. Tsultrim Tenzin, Dmitry Ermakov & Carol Ermakova. *Practice of Tsalung, Tummo, Thigle and Dispelling of Obstacles from the Mother Tantra*, (UK: FPYB, 2022 forthcoming).

Shenhla Wökar

i. Guru Yoga

You should pray to your Root Lama, offer mandala and beseech him to help you recognise your dreams as dream.

Visualise your Root Lama as Shenhla Wökar.[117] I think everyone is familiar with this peaceful deity. Don't think of your teacher as being just an ordinary person; think very strongly that he is a real Buddha. There is no need to check, no need to compare your Root Lama to Buddha and think that some qualities or something are missing. If you do, then your practice won't work properly.

ii. *Yidam* Yoga

You should offer *ganachakra* to your *yidam*, and *torma* to the *dakinis*.

a) Establishing the Boundary and Dispelling Obstacles[118]

Visualise your mind as a black HUNG / ཧཱུྃ.

Sparks emanate from this black HUNG. They look like sparks but they are in fact the energy of wisdom awareness. The HUNG emits many, many sparks which burn all external obstacles.

Sparks return to HUNG and dissolve in it.

HUNG transforms into Sangchog Tharthug Gyalpo. He has sixteen arms, and seven heads. In this case he is holding swords (not a skullcap of blood as in some pictures) with which he cuts off all inner obstacles. Inner obstacles are actually the main obstacles to practice – emotions such as anger, jealousy, pride and ignorance, as well as myriad discursive thoughts. Thinking a lot is not good for you. Nowadays, many diseases appear because people think too much. So you visualise Sangchog Tharthug Gyalpo with long swords which sever all inner obstacles. Everything is removed and becomes clear light.

---

[117] Tib. Gshen lha 'od dkar / གཤེན་ལྷ་འོད་དཀར།
[118] Tib. mtshams bcad pa / མཚམས་བཅད་པ།

Thus all inner and outer obstacles to Dream Yoga are purified.

While maintaining this visualisation, recite the mantra of Establishing the Boundary and Dispelling Obstacles. It is very important to main this visualisation properly, otherwise just reciting won't work.

b) Requesting Consideration[119]

One cubit above your head, clearly visualise Shenlha Wökar in a rainbow circle. If you can't visualise him, look at a picture again and again, then try to visualise him as clearly as possible.

The form is Shenhla Wökar but inside is your own Root Lama; your Root Lama appears as Shenhla Wökar.

In space in front of you, inside a tent of fire, visualise Sangchog Tharthug Gyalpo with his consort, Chyema Wötsö. She is red. Visualise this as clearly as possible. They are trampling demons underfoot, on a lotus cushion, as in the picture. This is your *yidam*. Don't think that they are flat, like a two-dimensional image. Your yidam is alive, made of compassion and wisdom, and his body is made of rays and lights, not flesh. There is nothing material – no gold or silver, copper or iron.

The external form is that of a wrathful deity, but inside is peaceful mind. You should visualise *yab* and *yum*[120] in union, as clearly as possible, while thinking that both Shenhla Wökar and Sangchog Tharthug Gyalpo with consort Chyema Wötsö are real Buddhas.

Then chant the recitation.

---

[119] Tib. dgongs gsol / དགོངས་གསོལ།
[120] Tib. yab yum / ཡབ་ཡུམ།

Sangchog Tharthug Gyalpo

Then go to:

c) Taking Refuge [121]
d) Generating Bodhicitta [122]
e) Prayer to the Lama and Khandro [123]

As you recite, do not let your mind wander. Focus strongly on Shenhla Wökar, Sangchog Tharthug Gyalpo and his consort Chyema Wötsö. Do not be distracted. This is very, very important.

f) Mandala Offering [124]

Visualise all universes, as many as you can. There are countless universes, not just our group. Visualise them as paradise.

Visualise all sentient beings – not just yourself or a few people, but all beings, everywhere – transform into gods and goddesses. These are offering awareness-holders and *dakinis*, not worldly gods or *devas*; they are all beyond this world.

All sentient beings, whoever makes trouble for you or whoever shows you loving-kindness, your enemies, your parents, birds, animals, worldly gods, hell beings etc. etc., they all appear as gods and goddesses.

The universe is full of many different things, and now these all transform into beautiful offerings, as a great mandala offering. The gods and goddesses gather up all these myriad offerings and proffer them to your lama, who is in the form of Shenhla Wökar.

While maintaining this visualisation chant the recitation.

---

[121] Tib. skyabs su 'gro ba / སྐྱབས་སུ་འགྲོ་བ།
[122] Tib. sems bskyed pa / སེམས་བསྐྱེད་པ།
[123] Tib. gsol ba 'debs / གསོལ་བ་འདེབས།
[124] In the text it is actually called Tib. bla ma'i dgongs spyod / བླ་མའི་དགོངས་སྤྱོད།

g) Contemplation

Imagine that a great wisdom fire emanates from Shenhla Wökar's body. The fire reaches you and burns all problems, negativities, illnesses and bad things, thus the two obscurations[125] and all defilements are burnt by this fire.

Then special water of wisdom emanates from Shenhla Wökar's speech and washes away anything that remains. Thus your mind and body become very clean.

Lights and rays appear from Shenhla Wökar's mind. Visualise that they dissolve into you. They look like light rays but by nature they are the Four Empowerments.[126] They come from Shenhla Wökar and dissolve into you. In this way, you receive empowerments and also all your broken *samayas* are repaired and purified.

This is very important.

h) Yidam Yoga[127]

Imagine that your body transforms into a *ganapuja* and offer it to Sangchog Tharthug Gyalpo. Then chant the recitation. But visualisation is the main point. You have already visualised Sangchog Tharthug Gyalpo in front of you in space, and now, as before, wisdom fire emanates from his body and burns all problems, diseases, mental sufferings, the two obscurations and all negativities. These are all burnt by this fire. And then wisdom water emanates from his speech as before. Imagine this.

Finally, rays and lights emanate from the *yidam*. Consider that with this, you receive all Four Empowerments from your *yidam*, Sangchog

---

[125] Tib. sgrib gnyis / སྒྲིབ་གཉིས༔: Tib. nyon mongs pa'i sgrib pa / ཉོན་མོངས་པའི་སྒྲིབ་པ། – emotional obscuration; Tib. shes bya'i sgrib pa / ཤེས་བྱའི་སྒྲིབ་པ། – obscuration of knowledge.

[126] Tib. dbang bzhi / དབང་བཞི༔: Tib. bum dbang, gsang dbang, shes rab ye shes kyi dbang, tshig dbang / བུམ་དབང་། གསང་དབང་། ཤེས་རབ་ཡེ་ཤེས་ཀྱི་དབང་། ཚིག་དབང་།

[127] Tib. yi dam gyi dgongs spyod / ཡི་དམ་གྱི་དགོངས་སྤྱོད།

Tharthug Gyalpo. Consider that any problems with your *samaya* are repaired.

This is *yidam* yoga. You should do this at the beginning of any session of practice. If you recite these three, *Gongchyo Namsum* at home every day, in the morning or in the evening then your mind will become more peaceful. Thoughts and the Five Poisonous Emotions will subside.

i) Khandro Yoga

Imagine your mind as a red syllable **OM** / ཨོཾ. This is the syllable of the *dakini* Chyema Wötsö.

Once your mind has transformed into a red **OM**, it exits from the crown of your head and transforms into Chyema Wötsö. She is holding a *kapala*[128] brimming with blood in her left hand, and a hooked knife in her right hand. With this sharp knife, she slices off the top of your head and puts it as a pot on a tripod fashioned from the three thousandfold universe. Then she chops up your body into many, many pieces, and places them inside the pot made from your skull.

Wisdom fire appears below the skull-pot and cooks the meat, your flesh, very well. As it cooks, it is transformed into amrita, *düdtsi*.[129] Then the *dakini* scatter this *amrita düdtsi* everywhere, to whomever needs it. They take this and are satisfied by the flesh of your body that has become amrita. The problems of whoever eats or drinks it are all purified and disappear. This amrita can remove all obstacles for them. Visualise this.

Then chant the recitation. But visualisation is extremely important. This is a short *chöd* practice. There is no *damaru*, but visualisation is very important. *Chöd* means cutting off attachments.

---

[128] Tib. thod pa / ཐོད་པ། – a skull-cap.
[129] Tib. bdud rtsi / བདུད་རྩི།

Visualise that many *dakinis* descend from all the ten directions and grant you blessings. They come down like rainfall.

This is how to practise the short way.

j) Prayer of aspiration[130]

Then you can recite the prayer of aspiration like a dedication.

Then remain in the Natural State for 10-20 minutes. Or for an hour. But 20 minutes is better. Like that.

This is the short version, but it is of very great benefit if you practise every day, in the morning or evening, whenever you are free.

If you do a retreat, you should practise this before every session, and before you go to sleep.

You should also perform the Four Generosities.[131]

These are:

Morning: *sangchö*[132]

Before midday: *chutor* – water offering

Afternoon: *surchö*[133]

Evening: *chöd*.

If you can, it is good to practise all four of these when you are doing a retreat. Otherwise, you can choose one which is convenient for you and practise that every day. If you do, you will have fewer obstacles

---

[130] Tib. smon lam / སྨོན་ལམ།

[131] Tib. sbyin pa bzhi / སྦྱིན་པ་བཞི། For more on this topic see: Khenpo Tenpa Yungdrung Rinpoche, Trnscr. & Ed. Carol & Dmitry Ermakovi, *Sangchö and Surchö: Teachings in Pauenhof, Germany 2005*, (Blou: Shenten Dargye Ling, 2008); Ermakov, D. *Be & Bön*, pp. 442-492.

[132] Tib. bsang mchod / བསང་མཆོད།

[133] Tib. gsur mchod / གསུར་མཆོད།

for your retreat, and if the landowners are satisfied, maybe they will help you with your practice.

Here are some words of Buddha:

> *'If you do not take the lama as Buddha and pray to your yidam, even if you visualise your yidam as clearly as possible, that is just your desire and will not bring much benefit.*
>
> *If you do not offer ganapuja to your yidam, even if you please the khandro, that is attachment.*
>
> *If you do not offer torma to the khandro, even if you practise and study with great effort, this is merely like a dog swimming.*
>
> *If you do not satisfy the wishes of the four guests, even if you realise yidam-body, that is merely grasping at attachment'.*

This means that if you want to practise Magyu, first you must consider your root teacher[134] as Buddha. Then you must offer him a mandala and practise *ganapuja*. You can either perform the large, extended *ganapuja* or do it the simple way, as I explained, by offering your body as *ganapuja*. In either case, visualisation is extremely important. If you just recite some text or mantra without clear visualisation, then even if you have a lot of offerings, recite many words and so on, it won't work well or be of much benefit. Visualisation is crucial. So you can simply visualise your *yidam*, offer your body as *ganapuja*, and if your visualisation is good, you can transform everything in the world into *ganapuja*. The last sentence in the quotation means that if you do not practise at least one of the Four Generosities, then even if you visualise your body as Buddha, this is merely attachment and of no benefit.

This was the teaching on *ngöndro*, Preliminaries

---

[134] Tib. rtsa ba'i bla ma / རྩ་བའི་བླ་མ།

Dream Yoga Preliminaries
Now we come to the Preliminaries for Dream Yoga.

There are four subdivisions:

i) How to sleep (posture)

ii) How to take refuge

iii) How to develop *bodhichitta*

iv) How to practise prayer.

i) Body Posture
Assume the sleeping lion position. This is the usual position of the Sleeping Buddha.[135]

Otherwise, there are three postures associated with the Three Poisonous Emotions – anger, desire and ignorance.

- Sleeping face down, lying on your belly is the posture of ignorance.

- Sleeping on your back is the posture of desire.

- Sleeping on your left side is the posture of anger.

If you try to practise Dream Yoga while sleeping in one of these three positions, you will not succeed. We call that an activity of delusion. Why? Because if you sleep on your belly, ignorance increases. If you sleep on your back, desire increases. If you sleep on your left side, anger increases. Therefore we call this the 'activity of demons.'

ii) How to take refuge
It is important to develop trust in the Three Jewels, i.e. lama, *yidam* and *khandro*. Your lama is your teacher. Your *yidam* is the deity which always resides in your mind. The *khandro* is *dakini*.[136] If you recite prayers or mantras without developing devotion or trusting the

---

[135] See illustration on page 8.

[136] Drubdra Khenpo explains: the word 'khandro' means someone who goes in space (Tib. mkha' / མཁའ་), but the real meaning in Bönpo Tantra is a female who has a profound understanding of the Natural State, and is consort to an awareness-holder.

Three Jewels, it is of very little benefit. Tibetans traditionally recite mantras and so on one hundred thousand times, but if you don't trust, merely reciting could even cause obstacles for you.

iii) How to develop *bodhichitta*

To develop *bodhichitta*, you should think that whatever you do is for the benefit of all sentient beings, so that they may achieve Buddhahood. If you practise a lot but think only of benefiting yourself, that is like an ambush, like hiding somewhere and shooting others. Therefore, whatever you practise should always be for the welfare of other sentient beings. That is *bodhichitta*. It is not for you, it is for others – your mother, father, friends, enemies, without distinction.

iv) How to pray

It is important to pray to the Three Jewels that you might recognise your dreams. If not, then your prayer is like slander; if you pray and pray but without any goal, then it is of no benefit. Therefore, when you want to practise Dream Yoga, it is important to pray to the Three Jewels and ask them to help you recognise your dreams as dream.

4. Special Preliminaries

There is another preliminary practice that is special for Dream Yoga. You should think of your body as *maya*, as illusion. I have already explained the Eleven Illusions, and you should think of your body in that way. You should have no attachment to your body. It is just like an illusion; you can see it, but it is devoid of inherent existence.

Before you fall asleep, you should visualise as follows:

- Visualise your Root Teacher, your guru, above the crown of your head. Consider him as Buddha.

- Visualise yourself as *yidam* Sangchog Tharthug Gyalpo.

- Visualise millions of *dakinis* all around your retreat place. They are all emanations of Khandro Gyuma Chenmo, the Khandro of Great Illusion. She has the following features:

She is standing in the dancing posture, similar to that of the *tsalung dakini*. In her right hand she holds a sharp hooked knife. In her left

Khandro Gyuma Chenmo

hand she holds a *gabala* skullcap brimming with nectar, and in the crook of her right arm is *khatamga*,[137] a trident, a three-pronged weapon that represents *yab*, her male consort. She is greenish blue, and adorned with many ornaments and jewellery, such as bone ornaments, and a headband of five dry skulls. She stands in a tent of fire. When you begin your retreat, you establish the boundary by placing a heap of stones in each of the four directions, i.e. East, North, West, and South. Now you visualise millions of emanations of Khandro Gyuma Chenmo all around your retreat place.

Do this before you go to sleep, and fall asleep with this visualisation.

Aspiration of taking dream as a path

You should develop the strong intention to recognise your dreams as dream. So all day long, you should keep silent, and if others are in retreat with you, you should not talk much to each other. Throughout the day, think again and again that whatever you see or do is a dream. Imagine that you are asleep and that everything around you is a dream. This is extremely important. You must generate this very intently, not just half-heartedly. Always. Constantly. Whatever you are doing – eating, drinking, everything – think that it is all just a dream.

This can change your karmic traces. What does that mean? The text says, if you are hungry, you think about food again and again, and so at night, you dream of food. In this way, you accumulate karmic traces in your *alaya*.[138] This means that because you thought about food all day, you accumulated those karmic traces in your *alaya*, and then at night, while you are asleep, these fresh karmic traces appear to you and you dream about food.

That is why it is important to meditate on all the four activities – eating, going to the toilet, sleeping, staying[139] – as dream. If you do

---

[137] Tib. kha tram ga / ཁ་ཏྲམ་ག

[138] Tib. kun gzhi'i rnam shes / ཀུན་གཞིའི་རྣམ་ཤེས – basic storing consciousness where all karmic traces are kept.

[139] Tib. za 'chag nyal 'dug / ཟ་འཆག་ཉལ་འདུག – eating, walking, sleeping, sitting.

this, then gradually it can lessen your desire and reduce your attachment.

Then, before you fall asleep, it is important to think again and again: 'I must have a dream tonight. I must transform that dream into the path.' In this way, you develop a very strong intention. Repeat this again and again.

Now there is a quotation:

> *'If you develop the intention to take dream as the path, go to sleep and then check: did I dream or not? Did I recognise my dream or not?*
>
> *If you did not have a dream or if you failed to recognise it, develop your intention again: 'I must have a dream! I must recognise my dream as dream!'*
>
> *Repeat this again and again, with stronger and stronger intent.*
>
> *Focus your mind on the* thigle.
>
> *There are four points:*
>
> *Remembering the channel, which is the location of the mind;*
>
> *Remembering the cause of all dreams, which is within the mind;*
>
> *Remembering the armour of the dream, which is the syllables;*[140]
>
> *Remembering the focus of dream, which is the* thigle.*'*

Firstly, don't think too much or let your mind wander as you are falling asleep. The mind should not follow after thoughts or agitation. Then visualise the central channel, in a similar way as in *tsalung* practice.

Secondly, here it says, 'without engaging in conversation, we should visualise smoke like a thin coil of incense smoke rising up the central

---

[140] This is explained in the next section below.

channel from the chakra of the secret place to the crown chakra. Imagine it fills the whole of the central channel. This smoke represents your mind, the Nature of your mind. It rises up and up, filling each chakra until finally it reaches the throat chakra.

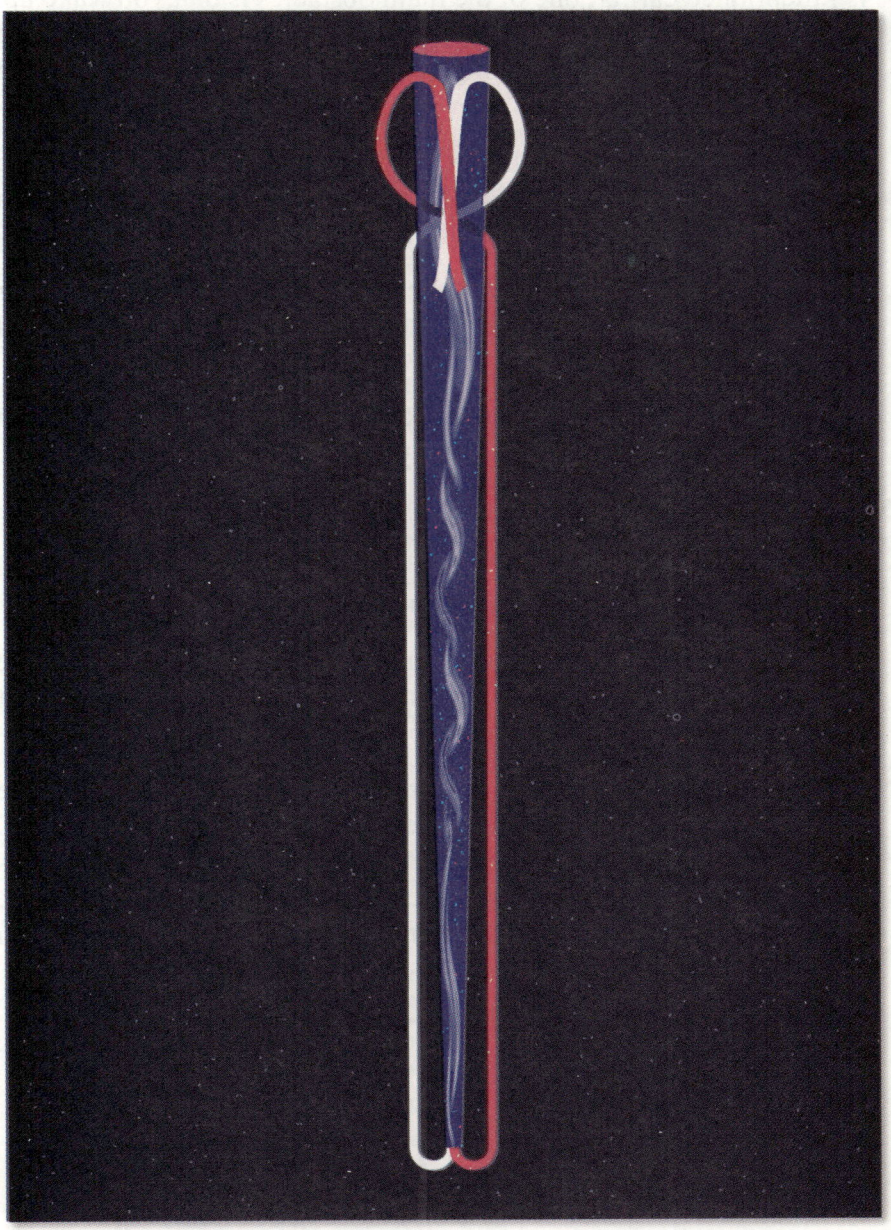

Visualisation of the three main channels for dream yoga

The Four Obstacles to Dream Practice

There are four main obstacles to practising Dream Yoga, so it is important to recognise these and remove them.

As I mentioned earlier, one of the main obstacles is that you wake up. Initially you fall asleep, you begin to dream but just as you start to recognise that you are dreaming, you wake up. This is a very big problem.

I mentioned the armour of the dream path which you need to don to keep you safe while dreaming. This is the armour of the *dakini*, which are represented by four syllables: RA, LA, SHA, SA.[141]

Each syllable represents a *dakini*, and each one is made up of four syllables combined, which means that they have a long, wrathful sound.

So for instance the first of the four, RA, consists of Ra, then a second Ra (wrathful), then Ha (augments), then hA (lengthens). This is the same for all four syllables.

How does one visualise this armour?

First, assume the sleeping lion posture I described earlier.

Then visualise the central channel as I taught previously. Visualise that the Nature of your mind is like smoke from a stick of incense that rises from the chakra at your secret place to your throat chakra.

In your heart chakra, visualise a red lotus with four petals. The syllables representing the dakinis are arranged as in the table below, with a red syllable A in the centre of the flower. Each syllables is standing vertically in the centre of its respective petal. Alternatively, you can visualise a small red thigle the size of sheep or goat dung in your heart chakra.

---

[141] See illustrations on pp. 57-60.

KHANDRO	SYLLABLE	ELEMENT	DIRECTION	POWER	BENEFIT/FUNCTION
Gyuma Chenmo	hA	water	above	Power of Life-force	Helps develop mind energy
Dagiye Drolma	YA	wind	below	Power of realization	Helps recognise dream
Tsogkyi Dagmo	RA	fire	east	Cutting	Helps cut off obstacles
Tharpai Lamdren	LA	water	north	Power of awareness	Helps remain aware while dreaming
Barchö Kundulma	SHA	fire	west	Power of the mind	Helps realise everything is as dream
Salgye Gödralma	SA	earth	south	Power of clarity	Helps clarify dreams

Khandro syllables RA LA SHA SA

Khandro syllables hA YA SHA SA

Heart chakra with syllables RA LA SHA SA, view from above

Heart chakra with syllables hA YA SHA SA, view from above

Since these teachings are from the *Sixfold Path of Magyu*, which is owned by six *dakini*, there are an additional two syllables: hA and YA. Thus if you prefer, you can replace RA with hA and LA with YA and visualise in this way instead.[142]

Here the text does not specify the colour of the syllables, although they generally correspond to the colour of the element they represent.

Then with this visualisation, pray to your lama, *yidam* and *khandro* to help you recognise your dream as dream, and go to sleep. That is the section on how to visualise before falling asleep.

Q & A Session

Q: Is the sleeping lion posture the same for men and women?

A: According to *Magyu* and *Zhang Zhung Nyengyu*, visualisation of channels, sleeping positions etc. are usually the same for men and women. The texts do not mention anything specific. In early times there was a very great Master, Drenpa Namkha, and he taught his mother Chyatsün Gungma[143] the text *Drenpa Chogdrug*.[144] He said to her: 'When you sleep, take the sleeping lion position and lie on your right side.' This is what Drenpa Namkha taught his mother, and since she was of course a woman, according to him there is no need to change anything. Some teachers may teach that the channels are opposite for men and women, but in my opinion there is no need for women to lie on the opposite side.

Q: Is there a special mantra for the *dakini*?

A: No. You can use the normal one:

བསོ་ཨོཾ་པུས་པ་ལི་དྷ་བ་རྫི་ལ་སྭཱཧཱ་ནི་རི་ཧཱུྃ་པཏཿ
SO OM PÜ PA LI DHA WA DHI LA SOHA NI RI HUNG PHAT

---

[142] See illustrations above.
[143] Tib. Phywa btsun Gung ma / ཕྱྭ་བཙུན་གུང་མ།
[144] Tib. Dran pa chog drug / དྲན་པ་ཆོག་དྲུག

Or you can use the mantra for lama, *yidam* and *khandro* together:

བསྒྲོ་ཨོཾ་ཨ་ཧྲི་མ་ཏི་ཌཱ་ཀི་ནི་ཧཱུྃ་ཕཊ྄༔

SO OM A HRI MA TI DHA KI NI HUNG PHAT

Q: What *samaya* vows should we take?

A: Generally there are many different *samaya* – five root *samayas*, a hundred branch *samayas* and then *bumde*[145] *samaya*, one hundred thousand *samayas*. In this case, it is as I said: you should consider your Root Master as Buddha, yourself as the *yidam*, and then visualising the *yidam* in space in front of you, offer mandala, *bumpa*,[146] *torma* and so on. You should visualise everything as the *yidam*. If you don't have a mandala or a *bumpa* and so on, you can simply visualise the *yidam* in space in front of you and recite the prayer to lama, *yidam*, *khandro*,[147] and especially the mantra of the *yidam*, with great trust and devotion. Then you should practice the *Gongchyo Namsum*, I explained earlier. If your devotion is interrupted or broken, that means you have broken your vow.

First of all you must know how to practise the Natural State. We say that the Natural State is *khandroi nyingthrag*,[148] the heart-blood of the *khandro*.

It is extremely important to keep these things and to trust the Three Jewels and then with this, to practise as much as possible. This is your *samaya*.

If your trust wavers or your no longer think of your Root Master as Buddha, or you forget your lama's teaching or the *khandro*, then you have broken your *samaya*.

---

[145] Tib. 'bum sde / འབུམ་སྡེ།

[146] Tib. bum pa / བུམ་པ། – ritual vase.

[147] See page 45.

[148] Tib. mkha' 'gro'i snying khrag / མཁའ་འགྲོའི་སྙིང་ཁྲག

Q: Can you tell us about *bönku kadag bardo*[149] please?

A: This occurs when your consciousness dissolves into your Nature and you can see your Natural State directly. You experience direct awareness at that moment. The Natural State appears to everyone in this first *bardo*, regardless of whether they recognise it or not. This is the 'Primordially pure body of *dharmakaya*.'

Q: Do we need to close our nostrils when we are in the sleeping lion position?

A: This is rather difficult. In some texts it explains that, when we are lying on our right side in the sleeping lion position, we should put our right thumb on the channel point in our neck, but you have to be very careful about this, otherwise if you press too strongly on this point, it can stop the flow of blood and you can die without realising it. You can also close your right nostril with your right ring finger, close your right eye with your right middle finger, and close your right ear with your right index finger. This can help to block the negativity of the channel, but it is rather difficult.

Main Practice – how to hold your dream

There are four key points:

i) The key point of inserting the prana-mind into the central channel

ii) The key point of clarifying the appearance of dream

iii) The key point of controlling the mind

iv) The key point of stimulating one's practice through fear.

Each of these has a further four subdivisions:

a) The four key points of time

b) The four key points of meditation

---

[149] Tib. bon sku ka dag bar do / བོན་སྐུ་ཀ་དག་བར་དོ།

c) The four key points of body posture

d) The four key points of the *dakini*.

If you are doing a Dream Yoga retreat, each night you should practise four sessions of two hours each. For example, from 10 pm – midnight; midnight – 2 am; 2 am – 4 am, and 4 am – 6 am.[150]

1*st* session

The **key point of time** is 10 pm – midnight.

The **key point of meditation** is the throat chakra. The text says that the throat chakra is the place where dreams are gathered and from where they appear.

The **key point of inserting prana-mind in the central channel** is through visualisation. So in this case, you should generate the same visualisation as I have already described, with a red four-petalled lotus. In the centre of the lotus, visualise a red syllable A.

The **key point of the body** is to assume the sleeping lion posture and try to fall asleep while maintaining the visualisation. Then you need to pray to lama, *yidam* and *khandro* that you will have a dream, and that you will be able to recognise it for what it is. You need to pray very strongly. Otherwise, sometimes you sleep without having a dream, but to practise Dream Yoga, you really need a dream! And it is not enough just for a dream to appear, you must recognise it as a dream, too.

The **key point of the** *dakini* is as I described earlier: you should imagine that the whole trichiliocosm[151] is filled with many, many *dakinis*, emanations of Gyuma Chenmo.

---

[150] For those countries where Summer Time (such as UK BST) is used, one should adjust this timetable accordingly to correspond with real time.
[151] Tib. stong gsum / སྟོང་གསུམ། or in full: Tib. stong gsum gyi stong chen po'i 'jig rten gyi khams / སྟོང་གསུམ་གྱི་སྟོང་ཆེན་པོའི་འཇིག་རྟེན་གྱི་ཁམས། – literally 'three-thousandfold great-thousandfold world system', is a universe of a billion worlds. For more detail see Ermakov, D. *Bө & Bön*, pp. 188-209.

This is how you should fall asleep.

As for the dreams, you may dream of a woman wearing abundant jewellery and ornaments who helps you ride on a *garuda* or a lion and guides you. You may dream of going up a mountain trail or up a ladder or stairs, perhaps to the roof of a house. Or you may dream that someone offers you a wish-fulfilling jewel or fruits such as apples or oranges, papayas and so on.

If you have this kind of dream and your visualisation is stable and you prayed properly to the Three Jewels, then you can recognise all this as a dream. *Milam* means dream, and dream is made by the *dakinis*. So if you dream of a lady, she might be Khandro Gyuma Chenmo. Therefore it is very important to pray to her sincerely.

These are just examples. You can dream of many different things, but the most important point is to recognise that whatever dreams you have – good, bad, neutral – are all just dreams, and that dreams are caused by Khandro Gyuma Chenmo.

The key point of the condition
a) Disturbed sleep
If your sleep is disturbed or too light, or you have a lot of discursive thoughts so that when you try to meditate, you can't because of agitation,[152] this could be caused by a disbalance of *lung*[153] (wind) energy or by poor food. In this case, you should eat rich food and massage your body with oil. Try to make your house and your bed warmer. Then go to sleep with the visualisation as before, and your condition should improve.

If you have good food, your room is warm and you do not have too much *lung* energy yet still you think too much, the antidote is to remain in the Natural State properly. That is a very good method.

---

[152] Tib. blo rgod / བློ་རྒོད།
[153] Tib. rlung / རླུང་།

Alternatively, you can do something strenuous until you are tired, and then when you want to sleep, agitation and thoughts will disappear.

Furthermore, some bad conditions could be caused by a provocation from negative spirits,[154] such as ghosts, demons, *nagas*, *nyen*, *sabdag* and so on. I had this very often in the past. I was sleeping and very much wanted to move my body and wake up, and although I could see everything very clearly, I was unable to wake up.[155] The doctor said this was a problem of blood circulation. Tibetans say that high blood pressure or suddenly falling unconscious (or having a seizure) is a disturbance sent from *za*,[156] a type of spirit. So if you have this kind of problem, or if you fall asleep and then suddenly feel afraid, it could be coming from spirits. In this case, you need to practise *chöd* to cut through the three illusions. The three illusions are: you, the spirits and all who harm you. *Chöd* is not just about reciting; the visualisation is very important. If you visualise and practise properly, then *chöd* is a good antidote to this problem.

b) Obstacle of not being able recognise dreams

If you can't recognise when you are dreaming or if a dream doesn't come and you sleep in a kind of darkness or dullness, this could be caused by an imbalance of the five elements. Our body is made up of the five elements:

- The body's heat is the element fire
- The breath is the element wind
- The mind is the element space
- The blood is the element water
- The flesh is the element earth

---

[154] Tib. gdon / གདོན།
[155] Tib. grib gnon / གྲིབ་གནོན།
[156] Tib. gza' / གཟའ། – planetary spirits or 'owners' who can cause seizures, epileptic fits, strokes etc. when displeased or disturbed,

If the elements are in conflict or disbalanced, or if we have poor blood circulation, this can cause darkness or dullness. You are asleep but you seem to be unconscious. If this happens, then you should practise *tsalung* or do some body exercise like *yantra* or *trulkhor*.[157] In this way, the condition of your body will improve. Why? Because through the practice of *tsalung* and *trulkhor*, the wind or prana circulate through your body better, thus problems and diseases are purified and things function properly.

2nd session

The **key point of time** is midnight – 2 am.

The key point of meditation. In your third eye, the spot on your forehead between your eyebrows, visualise a translucent white thigle the size of sheep dung or of a smallish bean.

The key point of inserting prana-mind in the central channel is to practise the wind practice with four aspects.[158] Repeat it seven times.

Then, as before, visualise yourself as *yidam* Sangchog Tharthug Gyalpo in union with his consort Chyema Wötsö and your Root Master above your head.

The **key point of the *dakini*** is as before: you are surrounded by many *dakinis*. If you don't have a dream during this time period or if you fail to recognise your dream as such, you must pray really strongly, with great devotion and intention.

You may dream that Khandro Gyuma Chenmo gives you the armour of the path. Or you may dream of the sun or moon rising, or of a dragon like a Chinese or Tibetan dragon, or you may dream you are blowing a white conch or gathering flowers or medicinal plants. You may dream of a bountiful harvest or of rich silk brocade, or of a white lynx. This kind of thing. Various sights, sounds, smells, tastes and

---

[157] Tib. 'phrul 'khor / འཕྲུལ་འཁོར།
[158] For details see D.K. Tsultrim Tenzin, *Magyu Tsalung & Tummo*, pp. 43-45.

sensations may arise in your dream, but it is important to recognise them all as dream.

This is the second session, from midnight to 2 am.

3rd session

The **key point of time** is 2 am – 4 am.

The **key point of meditation** is to visualise a black syllable **HUNG /** ཧཱུྃ in your heart, in the 'chakra of Bön.' If you do this, you will be able to control your mind.

The **key point of inserting prana-mind in the central channel**. Practise the wind practice with four aspects 21 times.

The **key point of the *dakini*** is as I described earlier: you should imagine that the whole trichiliocosm is filled with many, many *dakinis*, emanations of Gyuma Chenmo. Then maybe she will give you a dream as follows:

You may dream of a huge house that fills the trichiliocosm, that is so big that the whole billion-fold universe can fit inside. Or you may dream that you are staying in the mandala palace of the gods, that you are sitting on a very high throne, exalted in space, and are receiving teachings or something from your Root Master. Or you may dream that your father tells you to benefit sentient beings or that your mother offers you some delicious food. Or you may dream that you are sitting on cushions of lotuses, sun and moon discs on a throne supported by lions, like Shenhla Wökar's throne. But no matter what dreams you have, you should pray to lama, *yidam* and *khandro* to help you recognise everything as dream.

4th session

The **key point of time** is 4 am – 6 am.

The **key point of the body:** there is no need to take the sleeping lion position. You can sleep in any position that s comfortable for you.

The **key point of the mind:** the mind is free.

The **key point of meditation**: you should visualise something that frightens you. Why? Because this will act as a stimulus for your practice, a kind of encouragement. Then visualise a black *thigle* the size of sheep or goat dung in the secret place, in the hole from which urine exists. Focus on this and try to fall asleep.

The **key point of the *dakini*** is as before: you visualise many, many emanations of Khandro Gyuma Chenmo all around your retreat place, and the *dakini* will give you a dream:

Maybe you will dream of mountains, valleys or fields all on fire, burning. Or maybe you will dream of jumping into a lake or ocean and being carried away by huge waves, unable to swim. Or maybe you will dream of a very deep, narrow gorge or ravine, or that you are tumbling from a very high precipice. Or that a mighty wind – we call this the 'wind of destruction', that comes and the end of *kalpa*[159] – carries you away. Or maybe you dream that myriad rays and lights appear from your body, or that a wolf or tiger rips out your intestines, carries them off and eats them, or that a dog or jackal bites you. These dreams make you very frightened. These are dreams of the black *thigle*. You are really scared but then you think: 'oh, this is a bad dream!' So if terrifying dreams appear, it is easier for you to recognise that they are not real, merely dreams. And then the dream can't frighten you.

Thus if you recognise such dreams as dreams, then whatever dreams you have, be they good, bad or neutral, you can take them as the path to nirvana. All dreams are liberated into the path.

These are the four sessions you should practise during the night. However, if you prefer, you can choose whichever session is better for you, and use whichever visualisation best helps you have a dream and also recognise it as such. It doesn't matter whether you have a

---

[159] Tib. bskal pa'i rlung / བསྐལ་པའི་རླུང་།

good dream or a bad one, but it is important to recognise it as dream. If you have very good dreams but can't recognise them, then dream is dream, it makes you happy at that moment but is of no benefit. Bad dreams may make you frightened, but then you realise it's not so bad, you haven't died, it's just illusion.

So, it is very important to hold or recognise that dreams are dreams.

Training with the Wisdom of Dreams

When you train with frightening dreams it helps you develop and go beyond hope and fear. What is the wisdom of dreams? This means that you recognise all phenomena – whatever you see, hear, taste, smell, touch etc. – as illusion. Everything appears to you as illusion. In reality, in the waking state, nothing exists inherently, everything is just as in dreams. The Natural State is just emptiness with clarity. So whatever you see, hear, taste, touch, smell etc., be it daytime or nighttime, everything is mere empty form.

Empty form means that everything appears from awareness,[160] from the Natural State. The Natural State has three qualities: emptiness, clarity and unification. We talk about these three qualities, we use three different words, but the essence is the same. These qualities are inseparable, like water and wet, fire and hot. Therefore you should understand whatever you see during the day and whatever you dream during the night, good or bad, as illusion. In reality, nothing exists. Just empty form. With clarity. During the daytime you may have many thoughts, confusions, and realisation can't come from delusion. If you are deluded, you can't have realisation. But whatever comes – realisation or delusion – you can take it as the path. What does this mean? It means that you can transform everything into the path to nirvana.

For example, if someone is practising Tantra, then whatever comes, good or bad, they can transform it. They can change a very big mountain into Sangchog Tharthug Gyalpo for instance, and change

---

[160] Tib. rig pa / རིག་པ།

bad things to good things. This is a very important point; if you understand it, this is called 'wisdom.'

I have already explained the Eleven Illusions, and if you can understand everything as illusion, *maya*, then that is a very special practice. We say it is the unsurpassable path; there is no path beyond it. But even if there is no path beyond it, there is a shortcut nevertheless, a shortcut to nirvana! Nirvana is the opposite of samsara. If you go to nirvana, you have no suffering. You have a very special happiness beyond all suffering, happiness that can never change to suffering. That is nirvana.

During the daytime, it is very important to consider whatever happens as a dream. Imagine that you are asleep and that everything you do – eating, walking, playing football with friends – everything is all a dream. This is very important. As I told you the other day, if you think about something all day – for instance, you are hungry so you think about food – then that it is saved as a karmic trace. Dreams are karmic traces that are stored in the *alaya*. Fresh karmic traces appear more readily in your dreams, so if you discover the wisdom of dreams, that means that whatever appears, you know it is just a vision, inside your mind.

Throughout all the Three Realms,[161] everything is just like a dream. Nothing is really there, externally or inherently. At that moment, when you perceive it, it is just like a dream. Things seem very real in your dreams but in fact they aren't. Dream visions do not exist inherently, and it is the same during the daytime, too. Sometimes you need to think about this. Most people know that things change a lot, from summer to winter, for example, but if something existed inherently, it could never change.

---

[161] Tib. khams gsum / ཁམས་གསུམ།

So, liberate everything you see; meditate that everything is as dream. Train in this way. We call this *tsal*, or potential energy of wisdom.[162] For example, we usually consider thoughts or emotions connected with anger, ignorance, jealous and so on as 'bad.' But in fact, we can take them as the path to liberation, we can transform them, and so they have the potential energy of wisdom, wisdom awareness. This is the energy of wisdom.

Thus, you can take all things as the path, because everything is potential wisdom energy. You can transform everything so it becomes something positive. This is according to the teachings of Tantra. We have three vehicles or paths in Yungdrung Bön: Sutra, Tantra and Dzogchen.[163] The Sutra way is to remove or avoid all negativity. In the Tantra way, there is no need to remove anything because you can transform it and take it as the path. Why? Because everything is the cause of wisdom. This is called *lamchog*,[164] The Excellent Path.

You can train with this during the day by thinking that everything is just a dream. Then at night, even if you have a terrifying dream, for example, that you are surrounded by raging fire, you can think: 'Oh, no problem! I can jump into this fire and it can't burn me because it's just a dream!' Then you can even transform yourself into a huge fire and your body won't be burnt.

Similarly, if you dream of a river or water, you can recognise this is just a dream, that the river can't carry you away, and you can transform yourself into water, too. Then maybe you can offer some sentient beings your water emanation, and help them in this way.

Or you might dream of a very high cliff or rock face, or of a mighty wind or a forest of swords, or of dangerous ghosts or malevolent spirits, lords of death[165] and so on. Or you might dream of wild

---

[162] Tib. ye shes rtsal / ཡེ་ཤེས་རྩལ།

[163] Tib. mdo sngags sems gsum / མདོ་སྔགས་སེམས་གསུམ།

[164] Tib. lam mchog / ལམ་མཆོག

[165] Tib. gshed ma, 'chi bdag, gshin rje / གཤེད་མ། འཆི་བདག་གཤིན་རྗེ།

animals like tigers, leopards and lions. If you are able to integrate all these dreams as the path to liberation, that is the best path; no matter what you dream, you remain in the Natural State, and as you remain in the Natural State, you develop.

The next best practice is to transform whatever you see in your dreams. For example, you dream of a dog and transform it into a lion. If you recognise you are dreaming, then you can transform things in this way and emanate something that can benefit sentient beings.

But first of all you have to practise during the day until your practice is stable. If your daytime practice is not stable, then at night it will be extremely difficult to practise. If your daytime practice is stable, that is the base or foundation of Dream Yoga. If you train with Dream Yoga and are able to recognise your dreams, transform them and so on, then you can take dreams as the path. This is what it means to use dreams to go beyond hope and fear. You realise that everything is just illusion, *maya*, just like a dream, and so you can transform anything. In this way, you can go beyond hope and fear. It is very important. You must understand and know this.

Developing Dreams

What does 'developing dreams' mean? For example, if you dream of a man and you recognise you are dreaming, then you can think: 'Oh, this is man, it is a dream! I can emanate more!' And so you can keep doubling them – one becomes two, two become four and so on. This is developing dreams, or training with dreams. You can multiply anything – men, women, food, whatever. You can make one hundred, one thousand, one million or one billion even!

This is very similar to the *bardo*. If you recognise and remember this in the *bardo*, then whatever you want to change in the *bardo* is immediately transformed. You can change a man into Sangchog Tharthug Gyalpo or a woman into Khandro Gyuma Chenmo, and you can manifest hundreds of them. If you transform someone into Sangchog Tharthug Gyalpo, then you can request teachings from him!

The text we are using, for example, was written by a great master Milü Samleg, and he received this teaching from Gyuma Chenmo in a dream. So if you train and develop your dream practice, you can receive secret teachings from the *khandros*. It is like that.

Similarly, if you dream of wild animals that normally harm people, such as a wolf, tiger or a leopard – in the text it also mentions brown bears. In my hometown brown bears often harmed people and damaged their houses etc. in the summertime – if you recognise you are dreaming, you think; 'Oh, this is just a dream! The tiger isn't real, it can't hurt me! I can transform it into something else!'

Or you can emanate the great burial ground of Sangchog Tharthug Gyalpo – there are eight great cemeteries in the Magyu mandala – which is inhabited by many wild carnivorous animals that eat human flesh, but you can also emanate many *khandro* there and change all the impure things into pure ones.

Thus, no matter what dreams you have, you can develop and train in this way while you are asleep. This is Dream Yoga, real Dream Yoga.

If you become adept at this, then even in the daytime it will be no different. Visions or forms, whatever you see or hear etc. appears like a dream to you, even during the day. You will experience the Five Poisonous Emotions less strongly, you will have less attachment. Usually people are very much attached to whatever happens during the waking state, but actually that is very dangerous because it leads you deeper into samsara. If on the other hand you are able to consider everything as merely a dream, if you do this properly, then attachment will decrease. It is like that.

Sometimes you can hear the biographies of great masters and awareness-holders[166] who lived long ago, like Drenpa Namkha, Lishu

---

[166] Tib. rig 'dzin / རིག་འཛིན།

Tagring,[167] and Nangzher Lödpo.[168] These were all awareness-holders, or we call them *pawo*.[169] Female awareness-holders are called *khandro*, like Chöza Bönmo.[170] These people could emanate many things. For example, Drenpa Namkha could ride wild yak, or lions, tigers and leopards. He could control all these wild animals. In this text, it says that this is the result of practising Dream Yoga. If a master like Drenpa Namkha wanted to go out of his house, for instance, he didn't need to use the door, he could go through the wall. That is because he recognised everything as empty form. Dreams are empty, like illusions, and so here in the text it says that in ancient times, awareness-holders rode tigers or lions and travelled to Tagzig[171] – we call it Tagzig Olmo Lungring – or to the place where Tapihritsa was born. If you practise Dream Yoga properly, then as I said before, fire cannot burn you, water cannot drown you. If you train in this way again and again until you are able to control it very well while you are dreaming, then finally daytime and nighttime will be no different for you; the elements will not harm you. Nangzher Lödpo sometimes used to jump into fire and it couldn't burn him. Here, it says that is the result of Dream Yoga. Similarly, if someone cuts off your arm, you can reattach it to your body again. Weapons cannot cut or harm you. If you train with dreams until you are able to transform a bird into a *garuda*, ride it and fly though space, then the final result will be that you can ride a *garuda* through space during the day, too. This is the result of training properly.

Here follows a quotation from the root text:

> *'If you dream of fire, jump into it. If you dream of water, jump into it.'*

---

[167] Tib. Li shu stag ring / ལི་ཤུ་སྟག་རིང་།
[168] Tib. Snang bzher lod po / སྣང་བཞེར་ལོད་པོ།
[169] Tib. dpa' bo / དཔའ་བོ།
[170] Tib. Co za bon mo / ཅོ་ཟ་བོན་མོ།
[171] Tib. Stag gzig yul / སྟག་གཟིག་ཡུལ།

Q & A Session

Q: Can we recognise *rangjyung yeshe* in the dream state?

A: There are Six Paths in Magyu, and one of them, the sixth, is Sleep Yoga. Those teachings describe many visualisations but the main goal is to recognise *rangjyung yeshe* during sleep. Now I am teaching the Second Path, Dream Yoga. If you can recognise *rangjyung yeshe* in the dream state, that is best, but the main goal here is to change and transform your dreams.

Q: Should we use an alarm clock to keep to the 2-hour sessions?

A: Yes, you can use an alarm clock. In ancient times, when there weren't any clocks somebody else would wake up the practitioner, maybe an assistant or friend. Otherwise you might sleep the whole night through.

Q: What should we do if we can't fall asleep because doing the visualisation disturbs us?

A: That can be a problem at first. But slowly, slowly you will get used to it. If you practise *tsalung tummo* during the day and Dream Yoga at night then you will become the best yogi! Maybe like Drenpa Namkha!

The root text continues:

> '*If you dream of a woman, transform her into Khandro Chyema Wötsö and receive from her the Four Initiations.*
>
> *If you dream of a dog or wolf, transform it into hundreds of beasts in a cemetery. The cemetery is the mandala of Sangchog Tharthug Gyalpo.*

If you dream of a bird, transform it into garuda *and fly through space to the wish-fulfilling tree[172] from which you can see the whole universe.[173]*

If you dream of an elephant, transform it into Langchen Sasrung,[174] the elephant of Indra,[175] and visit the realm of the gods.

If you dream of a dog, transform it into a dragon, mount it and ride through space to all Three Realms:[176] Kamadhatu, Rupadhatu, Arupadhatu.[177]

If you dream of a snake, transform it into a naga, *mount it and travel to the* naga *realm, underground or in the ocean.'*

Obstacles to Dream Yoga

First you should train in recognising dream as dream, then once you are able to realise that you are dreaming while you are asleep, this is training with dream. But first you must practise very well, otherwise you won't be able to recognise that you are dreaming. Or sometimes you might realise that you are dreaming but forget to develop your training. These are what we call obstacles to Dream Yoga.

There are four great obstacles, *jyampa zhi*:[178]

---

[172] Tib. dpag bsam ljon shing/ དཔག་བསམ་ལྗོན་ཤིང་།

[173] Tib. Drubdra Khenpo explains: Mount Meru is the abode of many gods, and on the top of the mountain there grows a huge tree. Everything the gods need manifests from this tree. Sometimes Garuda perches on the tree, and so you can mount the Garuda and ride there.

[174] Tib. Glang chen sa srung / གླང་ཆེན་ས་སྲུང་། – white elephant with red head and six tusks

[175] Drubdra Khenpo explains: Indra abides on Mount Meru and is the great king of all the Thirty-Three gods there.

[176] Tib. khams gsum / ཁམས་གསུམ།

[177] Tib. 'dod khams, gzugs khams, gzugs med khams / འདོད་ཁམས་ གཟུགས་ཁམས་ གཟུགས་མེད་ཁམས། – the desire realm, the form realm and the formless realm.

[178] Tib. 'byams pa bzhi / འབྱམས་པ་བཞི།

1. Sejyam[179]

You begin to recognise that you are dreaming, but then you wake up.

2. Jejyam[180]

You get carried away by your dreams. For example, you recognise that you are dreaming, but you forget to train, so that if you dream of a woman, you forget to transform her into the Khandro or you forget to receive initiations from her.

3. Thruljyam[181]

Delusion. Although you have many dreams, you fail to recognise you are dreaming and don't train or develop. Instead, you just follow your dreams, getting more and more involved until it gets light and you wake up. Your dreams are no different from your waking state. We call this *thruljyam*, following deluding thoughts.

4. Gyujyam[182]

In the past, both in this life and in previous ones, if you didn't practise very well then your mind is always mixed with negative karmic traces. This is like oily paper. If you want to write on a piece of paper, you have to make sure it is clean first; you can't write on greasy paper. So if your mind is like oily paper, then it is obscured by karmic traces and you can't recognise that you are dreaming. When you dream, actions seem to take place; for example you might kill someone in a dream. When you wake up, the action is gone and nobody has actually been harmed, but the traces become obscurations or obstacles that prevent you from recognising dream as dream.

These are the four great obstacles to Dream Yoga.

---

[179] Tib. sad 'byams / སད་འབྱམས།
[180] Tib. brjed 'byams / བརྗེད་འབྱམས།
[181] Tib. 'khrul 'byams / འཁྲུལ་འབྱམས།
[182] Tib. rgyud 'byams / རྒྱུད་འབྱམས།

The Four Trainings[183]
This is similar to what came earlier.

1. Training with clarity
If you dream of the sun rising, consider it is the sun of dream. If you dream of the moon rising, consider it is the moon of dream. Remind yourself: I am asleep, I am dreaming, this is a dream moon. I can transform this any way I like. Think in this way. Then you can grab hold of the rays and lights emanating from the sun or moon and travel on them to the *deva loka*, to heaven.

2. Training with appearances
If you dream of a small cloud, you can change it into a multitude of clouds, catch hold of one and ride it to the *deva loka*, to paradise.

3. Training with objects of sound
If you dream of a dragon, roaring thunder and lightning, remind yourself: 'this is a dream! I can do anything!' Then you can catch hold of the lightning and ride the dragon to anywhere in the Three Realms.

4. Training with objects of vision
If you dream of a woman and you realise this is a dream, you can remember to transform her into a *dakini*. Then you can let the *dakini* guide you to Zhang Zhung or Mount Kailash or Tagzig, to Buddha's birthplace Olmo Lungring. Thus, you can travel anywhere, through space, and visit the realm of the Thirty-Three gods[184] on the top of Mount Meru. The text gives a lot of detail about this. Or if you want to visit Drenpa Namkha, you can let the *dakini* guide you there, and you can receive teachings from Drenpa Namkha or some other great master such as Tonggyung Thuchen.[185] You can request teachings on Dzogchen or Tantra, or initiations. Or you can visit *khandros* such as

---

[183] Tib. rmi lam gyi spyi don bzhi pa / རྨི་ལམ་གྱི་སྤྱི་དོན་བཞི་པ།

[184] Tib. sum bcu rtsa gsum lha gnas / སུམ་བཅུ་རྩ་གསུམ་ལྷ་གནས།

[185] Tib. Stong rgyung mthu chen / སྟོང་རྒྱུང་མཐུ་ཆེན།

Chöza Bönmo or Chyema Wötsö. There are many female *siddhas* in the Magyu lineage, in particular nine, *bönmo zungwa dgu*,[186] so you can visit them and request transmission, initiations, teachings and blessings in your dream visions.

Throughout the ten directions, there are Buddha places, and if we train with Dream Yoga, we can visit them. For example, in the fourteenth century there was a very great yogi called Shen Nyima Gyaltsen. He was of Tönpa Shenrab's lineage, and in the texts it says that he was always sleeping in his room yet travelling to the Buddha places everywhere.

There are also places where many *siddhas* gather to receive initiation from Drenpa Namkha or Tonggyung Thuchen, Drenpa Namkha's root master; these are the main *siddhas*. Sometimes they gather together in some place — we don't know where, but great yogis like Nyima Gyaltsen could go there, so if you become a great yogi of Magyu, you could go there, too, and do *ganapuja – tsog –* with *siddhas*.

So if you dream of a woman, you can transform her into a *dakini* and she will lead you to this place. We call it Khachyochyi Ne,[187] the place of *siddhas*. There are twenty-four special *dakini* places in the Magyu mandala, so you could visit them. There is one, Yang Lesho,[188] in the Kathmandu Valley, there are many special places, five Khandro of Magyu reside there, five tiger-headed Khandro, Tagdongma.[189]

Or you could visit Shenhla Wökar's place. It is very very far away, we say Ogmin,[190] and the *sambhogakayas* reside there, at the highest place, and teach great *bodhisattvas*.

---

[186] Tib. bon mo zung ba dgu / བོན་མོ་བཟུང་བ་དགུ།

[187] Tib. Mkha' spyod kyi gnas / མཁའ་སྤྱོད་ཀྱི་གནས།

[188] Tib. Yang le shod kyi brag phug / ཡང་ལེ་ཤོད་ཀྱི་བྲག་ཕུག

[189] Tib. Stag dong ma / སྟག་དོང་མ།

[190] Tib. 'Og min pho brang / འོག་མིན་ཕོ་བྲང་།

In the East, in space, is the Buddha realm known as Thriwö Karpoi Zhingkham.[191]

In the North is the Buddha realm known as Thrigyal Khugpi Zhingkham.[192]

In the West is the Buddha realm known as Mume Thayechyi Zhingkham.[193]

In the South is the Buddha realm known as Kunwö Dronmi Zhingkham.[194]

There are also special places where *bodhisattvas* are born and practise. We don't know where these places are, but the *dakinis* do. So if you train well with Dream Yoga, if you dream of a woman, you can transform her into a *dakini* and she can lead you to these wonderful places. She can guide you wherever you want to go.

There are also places in space where the *dakinis* gather to do *ganapuja*. So in your dream you could become like their leader or chief *dakini* and do *ganapuja* with them.

Or sometimes you could teach non-human beings such as *asuras*, demons, ghosts, spirits, *sabdag*, *nagas* and so on. The biographies of lamas from the distant past say that they could teach animals like brown bears, or birds like pigeons or vultures. This is the activity of *siddhas*, and it is also a result of Dream Yoga. So if you master this and practise very well, you will also be able to perform such activities.

Furthermore, in your dream you can meet dharma-friends – we say *yungdrung phundrog*[195] – to discuss and practise together. This is very, very important. You must keep your *samayas* with each other.

---

[191] Tib. Khri 'od dkar po'i zhing khams / ཁྲི་འོད་དཀར་པོའི་ཞིང་ཁམས།
[192] Tib. Khri rgyal khug pa'i zhing khams / ཁྲི་རྒྱལ་ཁུག་པའི་ཞིང་ཁམས།
[193] Tib. Mu med mtha' yas kyi zhing khams / མུ་མེད་མཐའ་ཡས་ཀྱི་ཞིང་ཁམས།
[194] Tib. Kun 'od sgron ma'i zhing khams / ཀུན་འོད་སྒྲོན་མའི་ཞིང་ཁམས།
[195] Tib. g.yung drung phun grogs / གཡུང་དྲུང་ཕུན་གྲོགས།

It is good to discuss practice, Dzogchen, the Natural State and Tantric teachings together, then you can discover who is a good practitioner or great yogi, you can develop your understanding and practice. It is important to discuss your *nyams*,[196] your experiences When you practise Dzogchen or other teachings, you can have some special experiences; if you practise a lot, you will surely have some realisation or experience, and sometimes it is better to discuss this with a dharma-friend; sometimes this is even better than talking with your Root Master, it can help your realisation develop. This is an important part of Dream Yoga.

Furthermore, if you dream of someone who has died, you should remember: 'Oh, this person is dead. This is a dream person, not a real human, so I can transform them.' In this way, you can go with this person and visit the Three Lower Realms[197] and maybe you will recognise somebody there, a friend who has died and is now in the hell realm or the hungry ghost realm or the animal realm. So then you can guide these beings who were once your friends and lead them to a higher realm. Also you can check and see for yourself what the Lower Realms are like, and you can teach the beings there. You can even teach Dzogchen to Shinje, the Lord of Death, The King of the Hell Realm.

This teaching is according to the Commentary by Milü Samleg.

Now there is a quotation from the root text, the words of Buddha. The meaning is the same, but the quotation is very condensed.

> '*In a dream, you can visit the Three Lower Realms and act for the benefit of sentient beings.*'

That is the explanation of this text.

---

[196] Tib. nyams / ཉམས།
[197] Tib. ngan song gsum / ངན་སོང་གསུམ།

Sublime contemplation[198]

Next the text talks about contemplation. There are three subdivisions:

1. Integration[199] – Integrate all appearances as dream; Integrate dream as *bardo*; Integrate dream as *wösal*[200]. As I told you earlier, I am teaching the second path from the Sixfold Path of Magyu. The final path teaches Sleep Yoga, and the phrase '*milam wösal*'[201] crops up very often. It means 'hold sleep as *wösal*.'[202] You often meet the term '*wösal*' in *bardo* teachings, too. Here, in Dream Yoga, it means we should integrate our dreams with Clear Light; Maya or illusion

2. Sublime contemplation

3. Cutting obstacles

1. Integration

Integrate all appearances as dream

As I explained earlier, you should consider all your daytime activities – eating, drinking, walking, driving, going to the toilet, reading, writing, everything – as a dream.

Similarly, you should perceive whatever you see, hear, taste, touch, or smell in the waking state, as a dream. No matter what you do – maybe you are a pilot and you fly a plane, or you are a train driver – you should integrate everything and see it as a dream. This is very, very important. If you think about this properly then when you go to sleep

---

[198] Tib. mchog gi dgongs pa / མཆོག་གི་དགོངས་པ།

[199] Tib. bsre ba / བསྲེ་བ།

[200] Tib. 'od gsal / འོད་གསལ། Drubdra Khenpo explains that since there is no direct English equivalent for this term, which can be roughly translated as 'clear light' or 'luminous light', it is good to remember the Tibetan word.

[201] Tib. rmi lam 'od gsal / རྨི་ལམ་འོད་གསལ།

[202] Tib. gnyid 'od gsal / གཉིད་འོད་གསལ།

at night it will be very easy for you to recognise your dreams as dreams.

If on the other hand you are always distracted during the day and never think about this, then you are just like a normal person, so if you try to practise Dream Yoga at night you won't be able to recognise your dreams as such. It will be extremely difficult to recognise that you are dreaming. Even if you visualise the red thigle on the four-petalled lotus and the four syllables before you go to sleep at night, it won't be helpful. It will be very hard for you to fall asleep, you will feel wide awake. Maybe you will do it tonight, tomorrow night, but after one or two weeks you will get fed up of this practice, so you will never realise Dream Yoga. That is why it is so important to always think that everything you do during the day – working in the office or in a shop and so on – is just a dream.

This is the first point, integrating appearances with dream.

Maya

You should think again and again, strongly, that whatever you see is an illusion, *maya*. Usually during the daytime everything seems very real, definite, but if you check, nothing actually exists inherently. There is no essence. We can see this very easily. Today, for instance, you may be feeling very happy, in a good mood, but then tomorrow that happiness is gone. It doesn't last long. Or today maybe you have some terrible suffering, maybe you even want to commit suicide, you're feeling really bad, but then after a while, you feel better. And then you might be happy again. So it is like this. Things change. And that shows that nothing is real, nothing exists inherently. That is *maya*, illusion, or like a dream.

Sometimes you might have a lovely dream, you are feeling very happy, laughing and smiling in your dream. But then when you wake up, it all disappears. It was just dream happiness. Or you might have a bad dream that makes you very sad. Perhaps you dream that your father dies or something. So in the dream you cry a lot, you are really sad. Your friend or somebody you are sleeping with hears you crying in your sleep, but if they ask you why you are crying, you realise it is just a dream, no reason to cry. It is the same during the daytime. You may feel worried or suffer, but if you check properly, you will see that in fact it is just an illusion, *maya*. Nothing is really trustable. It is like that.

Milam bardo

The Commentary says that if you fail to understand that all waking appearances (*nangwa*) are illusion (*gyuma*), then you will not be able to recognise your dream.

If you fail to recognise your dream, you will not be able to recognise *bardo* after you die.

We can be absolutely 100% sure that we will be in *bardo* after we die. Everybody dies.

If you fail to recognise *bardo*, then in the *bönnyi wösal bardo*,[203] the Bardo of Clear Light, you will again fall into the mud of samsara.

If you fall into the mud of samsara again and again, you may take rebirth in one of the Lower Realms and will have a very difficult time there.

Therefore, again and again, you should think that everything you do, all appearances and all activities, are as illusion, as dream or delusion.

If you think of this again and again without forgetting, then when you practise Dream Yoga at night, you will recognise you are dreaming.

If you recognise that you are dreaming, you will be able to recognise the *bardo* state. Most people don't recognise *bardo* as *bardo* and so they fall into the mud of samsara again.

Thus, this is excellent contemplation.

---

[203] Tib. bon nyid 'od gsal bar do / བོན་ཉིད་འོད་གསལ་བར་དོ།

2. Sublime contemplation

If you are able to recognise your dream as dream and all waking appearances as illusory, then samsara will disgust you. This is very important. Why? Because if you are very happy with samsara then you will not be motivated to practise well, you will not be able to go beyond samsara. If on the other hand you are fed up with samsara, you will be able to cut off your attachment. Attachment is very dangerous, it leads you deeper into samsara. The Lower Realms are places of great suffering. Now we are in the Upper Realms for a little while, and the situation seems better. But we should be disgusted by samsara, and then we have less attachment. If we have less attachment, then the Five Poisonous Emotions decrease, and *rangjyung yeshe*, the awareness of the Natural State, appears to us naturally.

Dreams are devoid of inherent existence, they are just empty form. Everybody knows this. If you eat honey in a dream, for example, you can taste, it is very sweet, but when you wake up, nothing is there. The sweet taste disappears. That means it is empty form. Like a rainbow. We can see a rainbow for a moment, but it won't last long. It soon disappears. That is empty form. Things look real but in fact they are empty. Dreams are like this, but it is the same in the daytime, too.

Dreams are not beyond our mind. What is a dream? Each of us has very many karmic traces stored in our *alaya*, and when we are asleep and our mind becomes clear, these karmic traces appear to our mind, and we see these things as dreams. That is why we say that dreams are not beyond mind. Dreams are integrated with our mind.

We can say that the mind is like an ocean, and dreams are like waves in that ocean. The waves cannot be separated from the ocean. The Nature of Mind is like this.

Therefore, nothing exists inherently. Rather, everything is mere empty form. Everybody should understand and become familiar with this.

Furthermore, if you understand appearances as *milam*, as dream, or illusion, then you feel disgusted by samsara and can sever attachment.

If you can do this, the demon of death is no more, and *rangjyung yeshe* appears.

Everybody knows the term *'rangjyung yeshe.'* You can even find it in the dictionary. But real *rangjyung yeshe* is inside us, it is our primordial wisdom. So if *rangjyung yeshe* appears, it naturally removes all grasping at the self – *dagzin*.[204] Usually we grasp very strongly at the idea of the self. For instance, if I am talking, I think that my talk is best. We are always thinking I, I, I. My, my, my. Me, me, me. This comes from grasping at self, at inherent existence. But if self-grasping disappears, that is Buddha! Buddha means no self-grasping. If you are Buddha, you can emanate the Three Kayas, Three Buddha Bodies.[205] These are the qualities of Buddha, but in fact the Three Kayas are all empty form. They look real, but their quality is Empty Nature.

This is a very good example. We always hear the word 'emptiness.' In Sutra teachings for example they always say *shunyata, shunyata*, but this is very different from what we mean when we talk about emptiness here.

The Nature of Mind is empty but it is also clear, clear to itself. It is not empty in the sense that something has been taken away or negated or that something is missing. This emptiness is beyond thoughts, we cannot express it in words. According to Dzogchen teachings, the Nature of Mind is clear by itself. This is very different from *shunyata* as it is understood in Sutra. In Dzogchen teachings, this Nature of Mind is empty, but also luminous. In *Zhang Zhung Nyengyu* it is written that when the sun rises, as it shines it illumines space, and we can see space with our eyes. It is like this. Empty but clear, luminous. Clarity is already present. If you look into your mind, it seems very empty. 'Empty' means that there are no characteristics, no substance, nothing. And yet it is very clear. Emptiness is like this. So here, this

---

[204] Tib. bdag 'dzin / བདག་འཛིན།
[205] Tib. sku gsum / སྐུ་གསུམ།

Empty Nature or Natural State is like that. Visions appear – forms, smells, things you can touch or taste and so one, we can think and do whatever we like – but they are all like reflections in water. The reflection of your face looks real, it looks like your face, but if you touch it, it is just water. Not your face. It is the same with the moon or anything else. So it is like this. Everything that appears is just like a reflection. Here, we can say that *rangjyung yeshe* is like water with reflections. You can think of it like that. *Tongpanyi*[206] – empty. Nothing is really there, no characteristics, no substance so it is empty, yet clear.

All the objects of our senses, everything throughout all the universes, first appears from *rangjyung yeshe*. Now they abide in *rangjyung yeshe*, and soon they will all disappear or dissolve into *rangjyung yeshe*, like salt dissolving in water. Now things don't seem as though they are empty, and that is self-grasping.[207] Self-grasping prevents us from seeing the real Nature. If you become a great *siddha* like Drenpa Namkha, you will see everything as Empty Nature. The text gives the example of arriving at an island of gold. If you go to an island of gold, everything is gold! There is no stone, everything is gold. So if you practise the Natural State very well, finally you will become like Drenpa Namkha and you will see everything as Empty Nature. This is excellent realisation. Perfect realisation.

This is very similar to the Dzogchen teaching. *Rangjyung yeshe* and the Natural State, awareness, are the same. If you remain in the Natural State, *rangjyung yeshe* is the same as Dzogchen, so you understand the quality and nothing is missing.

A practitioner of Tantra, however, can understand the Natural State, *rangjyung yeshe*, and awareness, but they don't completely understand the quality of the Natural State. They only understand part.

---

[206] Tib. stong pa nyid / སྟོང་པ་ཉིད།
[207] I.e. we grasp at the idea that things exist inherently.

That is the difference. But as for remaining in the Natural State, the Base of All,[208] without following thoughts, that part is the same.

Four Obstacles to Dream Yoga

I have already mentioned these briefly, but now the text gives more detail.

1. Thruljyam – Dreams of delusion

As I mentioned at the beginning of these teachings, we have six chakras and each one contains the seed syllable that represents one of the Six Realms of samsara. When you sleep, your mind enters one of these chakras, and the dreams you have correspond to the realm connected with the chakra.[209] So for instance, the seed syllable of the *asura* realm is in throat chakra, and the dreams are linked to their activities – fighting, brandishing weapons, wars like the First and Second World Wars, and so on. So you dream according to which chakra your mind has entered. But your mind doesn't always stay in the same chakra, it can move.

These dreams are called *thruljyam*, delusions. In past lives, these karmic traces were saved in the *alaya*, and now we see them as dreams. That is why they are called 'dreams of delusion;' they appear from your karmic traces.

Antidote: To cut off this type of dream, first you should practise impermanence and remember that nothing lasts for ever. Then, as I explained in detail earlier, during the daytime you should focus again and again on the fact that everything is as illusion, like a dream. This is the antidote to this type of delusion.

You should also recite prayers to your Root Lama again and again. Guru Yoga is another very good antidote. I think everyone is familiar

---

[208] Tib. kun gzhi / ཀུན་གཞི།
[209] See table on page 15.

with Guru Yoga. If you practise it well, not just once or twice but again and again, then you will receive what we call self-initiation.

2. Gyujyam

This means 'continuation of mind.' The meaning is not very clearly explained here, but I think it means that your mind is not stable, it is very easily controlled by the Five Poisonous Emotions. If your mind is muddled with the Five Poisonous Emotions, then it is very difficult to recognise your dream as dream. Even if you do recognise that you are dreaming, it will be very hard to transform your dream in the way I explained earlier. It will be difficult to develop your dream by transforming whatever appears in your dream.

Antidote: The antidote to this obstacle is to practise confession. How can we do this? The Magyu teachings contain a special mantra recitation whereby you visualise Shenhla Wökar or Sangchog Tharthug Gyalpo or Khandro Chyema Wötsö or Lama, *Yidam* and *Khandro*, and then you visualise that wisdom water emanates from them and washes away all your negativities and obscurations. Do this again and again.

Alternatively, you can visualise your Root Lama. Sometimes in the monastery, Yongdzin Rinpoche[210] gives us *trü*.[211] This is water mixed with saffron or camphor. The monks recite a lot of mantras for a long time and then blow on this water, and so the water becomes blessed, and useful for purification. If you practise this purification and visualise your Root Master, that is of great benefit.

Why do we need to practise purification and confession? As I told you the other day, our mind is like oily paper, it is mixed with the Five Poisonous Emptions and so first we have to know how to clean it a bit. If you want to write on a piece of paper but the paper is greasy,

---

[210] I.e. Yongdzin Lopön Tenzin Namdak Rinpoche / ཡོངས་འཛིན་སློབ་དཔོན་བསྟན་འཛིན་རྣམ་དག་རིན་པོ་ཆེ།
[211] Tib. khrus / ཁྲུས།

first you have to clean it, you need to remove the oil. Then you can write whatever you want. It is like this.

3. Sejyam

I have already mentioned this obstacle to Dream Yoga. When you are asleep and just beginning to recognise that you are dreaming, you suddenly wake up. This is a big obstacle for Dream Yoga. The text says that this problem arises because the *dakinis* do not like you because you made a mistake. They are displeased. If the *dakinis* are not happy with you, then even if you practise Dream Yoga very diligently, you will not be able to recognise when you are dreaming.

Antidote: If there is a fault or a fissure in your *samaya* with the *dakinis*, then you must confess your broken *samaya* and repair it by offering *ganapuja* and invoking the *dakinis*. You should offer many good things, with great devotion, and apologise very sincerely.

4. Jejyam

If you recognise that you are dreaming, then in this lifetime you can obtain ordinary *siddhi* such as clairvoyance and the ability to emanate many things. In the *sipi bardo*,[212] the Bardo of Existence, it is very important to recognise this state as *bardo* and to remember. If you are able to recognise when you are dreaming, that is of great benefit. If you are able to recognise the *bardo* state, then you can remember your practice. If you remember to remain in the Natural State in bardo, then that is of really great benefit, maybe 100 times more beneficial than remaining in Nature during this lifetime. Why? Because if you recognise and remain in the Natural State in *bardo*, then it is very easy to become a Buddha. You can sever your desires and attachments, and once you have cut them, you will not re-enter *bardo* unless you choose to.[213] That means you become a great awareness-holder like Drenpa Namkha; an awareness-holder never falls back into samsara, and in the next life you can realise the Three Kayas – *dharmakaya*,

---

[212] Tib. srid pa'i bar do / སྲིད་པའི་བར་དོ།
[213] E.g. in order help beings etc.

sambhogakaya and *nirmanakaya* – the three Buddha forms or bodies. If you realise the Three Kayas, then you can act for the benefit of sentient beings because you have achieved Buddhahood.

Result

I have already explained *thruljyam* obstacle to Dream Yoga. If this obstacle is removed, then you will undoubtedly recognise the *bardo* when you arrive there.

Segyam – if you cut off this obstacle, then you will be able to achieve the Three Kayas in your next life.

If you sever the obstacle of forgetting to transform your dream, *gyujyam*, then this is like a wish-fulfilling jewel, you will be able to benefit sentient beings.

These are the words of Buddha Kuntu Zangpo Shenhla Wökar, *dharmakaya*, who is blue, and naked. Shenhla Wökar is adorned with many ornaments etc. Shenhla Wökar is also called *dharmakaya* Kuntu Zangpo. As I explained earlier, for the Magyu preliminary practices, it is very important to visualise Shenhla Wökar above your head. His nature is that of your Root Lama and his form is that of Shenhla Wökar. Even if you visualise Shenhla Wökar very well, if you do not have devotion to your Root Lama or hold him in high esteem, then your practice will not develop well, something is wrong. Thus it is paramount to consider your Root Master as Buddha, in the form of Shenhla Wökar.

This teaching appeared from Kuntu Zangpo Shenhla Wökar, who taught it to Khandro Gyuma Chenmo, from whom Milü Samleg received it. Milü Samleg wrote down this Commentary. The root text is the words of Buddha. Milü Samleg practised very well, he was an excellent practitioner and obtained very great *siddhi*. He wrote down this Commentary, and its blessings are equal to those of the Buddha's words.

Excellent realisation.

There are a total of 30 subdivisions in this text.

Sealed! Sealed! Sealed!

This teaching is very secret; do not tell it to people who are not connected to the teachings of Tantra or to those who are not devoted to Yungdrung Bön.[214]

Q & A Session

Q: How do we visualise the *yidam*?

A: We talk about three *sempas*,[215] mind-heroes or *bodhisattvas*. You visualise your body as your *yidam*, as Sangchog Tharthug Gyalpo. That is what we call *damtsig sempa*,[216] *samayasattva* or *samaya* being.

The actual Sangchog Tharthug Gyalpo, the wisdom *bodhisattva*,[217] resides in paradise or heaven, so you visualise sending rays and lights up to this Sangchog Tharthug Gyalpo. The rays and lights reach him and touch him and he kind of wakes up. When you visualise rays and lights returning to you, that is his blessing. By these rays and lights, you are inviting the actual *yidam* to come to your visualisation, your *damtsig sempa*. Finally, the actual Sangchog Tharthug Gyalpo transforms into lights which dissolve into you. Thus your visualised

---

[214] One may ask: 'Then why is this teaching made public here?' Drubdra Khenpo explains that nowadays everything is openly available as books or on the Internet so in order to counteract wrong translations or interpretations, this teaching is offered publicly. Nevertheless, as mentioned in the Foreword, to practise these methods correctly and achieve the result, one must receive transmission, authorisation and further instructions from an authentic Bönpo lama to become connected to the transmission lineage and receive the empowering blessings (Tib. sbyin rlabs / སྦྱིན་རླབས།) without which one will not be able to obtain real knowledge or realisation.

[215] Tib. sems dpa' gsum / སེམས་དཔའ་གསུམ།

[216] Tib. dam tshig sems dpa' / དམ་ཚིག་སེམས་དཔའ།

[217] Tib. ye shes sems dpa' / ཡེ་ཤེས་སེམས་དཔའ།

yidam and the actual *yidam* in paradise have the same quality. And this third stage is called *nyime lechyi sempa*,[218] non-dual *sempa*.

Q: Will you give us permission to practise and *lung*, transmission?

A: I give you permission to practise. I have already taught everything, and I think that if you practise, this is enough for the moment.

The best Dream Yoga is to recognise your Natural State, your awareness, when you are dreaming. If you can recognise your Natural State when you are asleep and remain in it, then there is no need to transform your dreams as I described earlier; remaining in Nature is enough.

---

[218] Tib. gnyis med las kyi sems dpa' / གཉིས་མེད་ལས་ཀྱི་སེམས་དཔའ།